DR ZOE WILLIAMS

YOU GROW GIRL!

THE COMPLETE NO WORRIES GUIDE TO GROWING UP

ILLUSTRATED BY
LUNA
VALENTINE

YOU GROW GIRL!

I dedicate this book to the two women in my life who always told me, 'YES, YOU CAN' — my mum, Marilyn, and my PE teacher, Lil Dykes.

First published in Great Britain in 2023 by Wren & Rook

ISBN: 978 1 5263 6515 6
eBook ISBN: 978 1 5263 6516 3

10 9 8 7 6 5 4 3 2 1

MIX
Paper from
responsible sources
FSC® C104740

FSC
www.fsc.org

Wren & Rook
An imprint of
Hachette Children's Group
Part of Hodder & Stoughton
Carmelite House
50 Victoria Embankment
London EC4Y 0DZ

An Hachette UK Company
www.hachette.co.uk
www.hachettechildrens.co.uk

Printed in China

CONTENTS

INTRODUCTION

WELL, HELLO THERE . . .

and thank you so much for picking up this book. In these pages you will find everything you have ever wanted to know about puberty, growing up and developing the confidence to become the very best version of yourself. During puberty, your body starts growing at a much faster pace – in fact, the only time it grows faster is when you are a baby. It's not surprising, really, as puberty is when your body matures from child to adult.

You may have siblings who have already gone through puberty so this might be something you're already familiar with, or it might be completely new to you. But even if you've never heard the word puberty before, don't fear, because within these pages you will discover everything you need to know about growing from a girl into a woman.

This might initially seem a bit scary and confusing, but I'm going to help answer all the questions that might be filling your head right now. We'll look at how your body, your feelings and your relationships might change as you grow up. We'll learn everything you need to know about periods, hormones and how to look after your health. And we'll make sure that whatever stage you're at, you'll be left feeling confident, informed, positive, prepared and maybe even a little excited about what's going on.

And this book's not just about the physical stuff either. I want you to feel empowered to talk about your mental health, to be equipped to navigate healthy relationships and to leave feeling armed with all the knowledge you need to flourish and thrive in today's world.

But first things first, I should start off by telling you a little bit about myself. Well, I'm Zoe. I'm a doctor, a TV presenter, a mother and an athlete. And a few years ago, I was also a gladiator! (Yes, you heard it right!)

But one thing I've learned is that life is a rollercoaster and comes with lots of ups and downs. Growing up, I was actually extremely shy and I had severe asthma, which regularly landed me in hospital and also meant that I missed quite a lot of time at school. It made me fearful of many situations. My parents divorced when I was very young, and my mum, brother and I struggled financially. I was also the only black girl at my school, so I constantly felt like the odd one out and was always aware, especially with my afro hair, that I looked different. So this, coupled with the biological and emotional changes we all experience during puberty, means that I know all about how hard growing up can sometimes be.

But I got through it and went on to achieve my dreams. And I know you will too. My favourite mantra is

YES, I CAN!

And I genuinely believe that everyone has the potential to do whatever it is that they want to. So by the end of *You Grow Girl*, I hope you will feel empowered to work hard, aim high and believe in yourself, as that is the recipe for living your best life while negotiating the ups and downs of puberty with style and confidence.

As you work your way through this book, you'll notice that there are little prescription notes in each chapter – what can I say, once a doctor, always a doctor! But these aren't prescriptions for medicine, they're for actionable tasks and advice that you can apply to your life and try at home.

Oh, and there are a few overshare moments too, cos we all make mistakes, and none of us get it right all the time. I hope these make you laugh, cry, sigh or give a knowing nod!

So, shall we get started?

CHAPTER 1

PUBERTY, AKA WHAT IS HAPPENING TO MY BODY?!

First things first, what even is puberty? Well, in a nutshell, puberty is when your body transitions from being a child's into an adult's. This is a **MASSIVE** thing, so it's not at all surprising that it can feel like a physical and emotional rollercoaster.

Puberty usually starts between the ages of eight to thirteen in girls and nine to fourteen in boys. If a girl starts showing signs of puberty before eight, it's called early puberty and it's recommended that she see her GP. If you think this is happening to you, ask a parent, carer or other trusted adult to help you contact your doctor.

Nobody can tell you exactly what your experience of puberty will be like because it's completely different for each and every one of us, and it can be both a wonderful and challenging time. But I am here to reassure you that you will get through those challenges and you can come out the other side feeling happy and confident with the person you've become.

During puberty, you will notice things about yourself and those around you changing – from the way you look and feel, to the different relationships you have with people. In this chapter I'm going to talk you through the physical changes happening in your body. I'm a firm believer that knowledge is power, so once you have a better understanding of what's happening to you physically, you'll feel fully equipped to handle those changes, and you will have a better understanding of any emotional changes you might experience too. This is one of my main reasons for writing this book, as I so wish I'd had this kind of information when I was growing up!

Hormones

Speaking of emotional changes, you may have noticed that your mood has already started swinging up and down and all around. One minute you're on top of the world and the next it feels like the end of the world! Please don't worry; this is perfectly normal. Let me repeat that in upper case for emphasis: **PLEASE DON'T WORRY; THIS IS PERFECTLY NORMAL!** Mood swings during puberty are mainly caused by chemicals known as hormones – be warned, you'll be getting to know these guys very well throughout this book.

Once girls enter puberty, they begin producing much more of a hormone called oestrogen, and boys begin producing more of a hormone called testosterone. These hormones cause your body to start changing in several different ways. We are all perfectly unique, so we will experience changes to different extents to other people. Here are some pictures to show how your body will change . . .

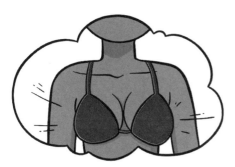

BREASTS – you will start to develop breasts and your nipples will get larger

SKIN – increased sebum (oil) production in the skin can cause skin and hair to feel greasier and can cause acne on the face, neck, chest and back

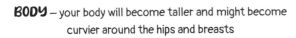

BODY – your body will become taller and might become curvier around the hips and breasts

PERIODS – you will start your menstrual cycle

STRETCH MARKS — as your body grows, some thin streaks might appear on your skin

ARMPITS/PUBIC AREA — you will grow hair here and the sweat glands become active in these areas, which can cause body odour

ARMS and LEGS — you will grow more hair here too

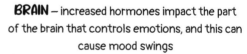

GENITALS — your vulva will grow larger

BRAIN — increased hormones impact the part of the brain that controls emotions, and this can cause mood swings

Skin

Spots

So you wake up one day and **OH MY GOD, WHAT IS THAT MASSIVE VOLCANO ON YOUR FACE?!** We've all been there. Spots. They appear when you least expect it and usually when you have something really exciting planned, as if they've been cunningly waiting just so they can ruin your day. But first things first, you will always think spots look worse than they actually do. And secondly, spots are really very common in puberty, so you are not alone.

They happen due to the hormonal changes which stimulate oil glands. The follicles (or pores) in your skin expand and get blocked with oil and dead skin cells. Some spots can appear white – known as whiteheads –

and some can be black – known as, surprise surprise, blackheads. Sometimes the bacteria that live on the skin cause inflammation, and the spots can get red and sore.

Acne

Acne is the name of the condition where people have lots of spots. It is very common – in fact, eight out of every ten teenagers will have acne at some point. It usually doesn't last into adulthood, with most people growing out of it after four or five years. Typically, people tend to get acne on their face, but it can also crop up in other places, like the neck, chest, back, shoulders and buttocks. Breaking out in acne can be really upsetting but there are several things you can do to help keep it at bay – and the best news is, they're a whole lot simpler than the recommendation from a doctor named Daniel Border back in 1651, who suggested that people rub their spots with the hand of a dead man to make them disappear! Here are a few of them:

1. **Cleansing.** The most important thing when it comes to spots and acne is cleansing your skin. It's really important to cleanse well twice a day, morning and night, with a gentle cleanser or face wash. But don't wash too much or use harsh soaps and scrubs as this can trick the skin into thinking it's too dry, so it produces more oil, meaning more spots. And this may sound strange given that oil causes spots, but it's also really important to moisturise your skin too, as this acts as a barrier

and protects it. If you've got oily skin or get a lot of breakouts, use an oil-free moisturiser and choose gels over creams. I know it can sometimes be tempting to leave your make-up on when you go to bed, but to help avoid spots, make sure you remove it every night. If you can't be bothered to go to the sink, remove make-up with micellar water rather than face wipes and avoid oil-based cosmetics (you can check on the label to make sure they're oil-free).

2. **Don't pick or scratch!** However tempting it might be, it's also really important to avoid picking or scratching at spots as this can lead to more inflammation and permanent scarring. This is even more important if you have skin of colour as it can scar more easily. Using sunscreen helps to reduce the dark marks that remain after a spot. Also, try not to touch your face or sit with your hands on your face during the day as this can transmit bacteria from your fingers. It's worth thinking about what products you put on your hair too, as we tend to touch our hair a lot, then our face. If you need to use oily products on your hair, like I do for my afro hair, then even more reason to break the habit of touching your face.

3. **Fuel your skin.** I've known many friends and patients who spend a fortune on fancy creams and potions for acne, but the truth is sometimes the biggest changes are made when you fuel your skin cells the right way, through what you eat and drink.

Good hydration is vital as it helps the body remove toxins and can reduce inflammation, and a diet full of colourful fruits and veggies gives your skin all the vitamins and nutrients it needs. Healthy fats, like olive oil, avocado, nuts and oily fish also support good skin health.

4. **Over-the-counter treatments.** If a healthy diet and regular cleansing don't work, you can get an over-the-counter treatment for acne from your local chemist, so ask your parent or carer to take you. The pharmacist will be able to give you professional advice for free, and no appointment is needed. Treatments like benzoyl peroxide, which reduces the bacteria on the skin, can be bought over the counter as long as you're over twelve. Most treatments need to be used for up to eight weeks to be effective. Many people don't know this, so a common mistake is to give up too soon. It's also important to know that these treatments can cause some dryness, mild irritation and redness at first, but this usually settles after the first week, so just use a tiny amount at first and remember to use a moisturiser. If the dryness and irritation are mild, it's worth sticking with it. You may need to try a few different ones to find a good match, and look out for ingredients such as salicylic acid and AHAs, which further help remove dead skin cells. Make sure you massage well to unclog your pores, but avoid picking and peeling the skin if it's flaking.

5. **See your GP.** If these options don't work, I'd recommend you make an appointment to see your GP to discuss the many other treatments that can be prescribed, and if at any time you start developing big, painful under-the-skin spots that don't always come to a head (we call these nodules and cysts) then see your GP as these can cause scarring. Remember, while acne is absolutely normal during puberty, it can be treated, so if you're seeing scarring – see your GP.

MYTH BUSTER

There's a common myth that chocolate makes acne worse. This isn't completely true, as it doesn't show the full picture. High sugar, dairy and high-fat foods (including chocolate) have been linked to increased acne, but other foods such as oily fish, fruit and vegetables are protective against acne. So as long as you're keeping your body well hydrated and eating a healthy, balanced diet, then the occasional sweet treat won't cause you to get spots. There's more on diet later in the book.

Dr Zoe's Prescription

+

Be kind to your spots

I didn't have that many spots during puberty, but whenever I did get them I'd really focus on them and pick at them and beat myself up in the mirror. If this sounds like you, I have a great exercise for you. Take some time to look at your face in the mirror and imagine that those same spots were on your best friend's face. How would you feel about them if they weren't yours? And what would you think about them being there? Would your friend having these spots change the way you think about them? I'm guessing not. We tend to be way more negative about our own appearance than we are about others', and we tend to be way kinder to others than we are to ourselves.

My challenge to you is to treat yourself – and your spots – with the same kindness you'd show to a friend and theirs.

To complete this exercise, choose three things that you like about yourself and focus on them instead, saying them out loud or in your head like a mantra. For example: I really like my hair. I really like my eyes. I really like my body's strength.

Stretch marks

Another really common effect of puberty on your skin is getting stretch marks. Stretch marks are indented thin streaks on the skin that can appear pink, red, brown, black, silver or purple. **THEY ARE NORMAL** and most people have them. They usually start off more obvious and fade with time. They tend to appear on our skin after a period of rapid growth and are sometimes down to hormones.

During puberty, you are most likely to get stretch marks on your breasts or hips. They often fade but not always. Occasionally they can cause some discomfort if the skin is very thin in that area, so it's best to keep them well moisturised as this can help to strengthen the skin barrier.

I have stretch marks on the sides of my hips and the fleshy parts of my thighs, and I've always liked them. Maybe it was because I started my periods later than my friends and I was the last of us to get stretch marks. I was so happy when they did finally arrive because I saw them as a sign of growing up and maturity. I call them my tiger stripes. So if you've got stretch marks appearing on your body, I challenge you to celebrate your tiger stripes too!

MYTH BUSTER

A lot of women think that the vagina is the name for the female genitals, but the vagina is actually only half of the story – the internal half – referring to the inner passage linking the external genitals to the uterus. So, without further ado, allow me to introduce you to your external genitals – the vulva!

VAGINAL OPENING – this is where to insert a tampon or menstrual cup, where a penis is inserted during vaginal sex, and also from where a baby enters the world in a vaginal birth (some babies are born by an operation called a caesarean section, through a cut in the lower abdomen)

CLITORAL HOOD – protects the clitoris from irritation and unwanted stimulation

CLITORIS – well, actually this is the glans clitoris, the most sensitive part of the clitoris, and the only part which can be seen in the vulva – the rest of this wonderful organ is internal

MONS PUBIS – this is the area at the bottom of the belly, where hair grows at puberty

URETHRAL OPENING – this is where you pee from – a tube called the urethra connects this small opening to the bladder

LABIA MAJORA, OR OUTER LIPS – these become covered in hair and are there to protect the rest of the vulva – labia is Latin for lips

PERINEUM – this is the name given to the area of soft tissue between the anus and vaginal opening

LABIA MINORA, OR INNER LIPS – these are a second line of protection and can vary in size and shape a lot from person to person, just like the lips on faces do

ANUS – this is not part of the vulva, but labelled here to show its proximity

Hair growth

During puberty, hair starts sprouting in unfamiliar places, especially your armpits and pubic area (this is called pubic hair), and this can make you quite self-conscious.

What should I call it?

Before we go any further, I think we need to address the elephant in the room – what exactly should us women and girls call our genitals? Perhaps because their genitals are all on the outside of the body, boys have no problem naming theirs – the penis and the testicles. But for girls it's slightly more complicated, because the external genitals are called the vulva and the internal genitals are called the vagina.

As well as starting to grow pubic hair, during puberty the vulva gets larger. But lots of women and girls don't feel like they know what their vulva looks like because it is not that easy to see without a mirror.

It's a good idea to look at your genitals in a mirror every now and then. The better you know your body, the more comfortable you will feel about it and the better you can look after it. Find somewhere comfortable and private and place a hand mirror between your legs, moving it around so you can see exactly what your vulva looks like. See if you can identify your labia majora and mons pubis – these are the areas where you will first see pubic hair growing.

We own our bodies — they are ours to look at, understand and look after, so never feel that there is anything rude or wrong with knowing what your entire body looks and feels like. Getting to know your body is a skill, so practice makes perfect. All vulvas look different and are equally amazing.

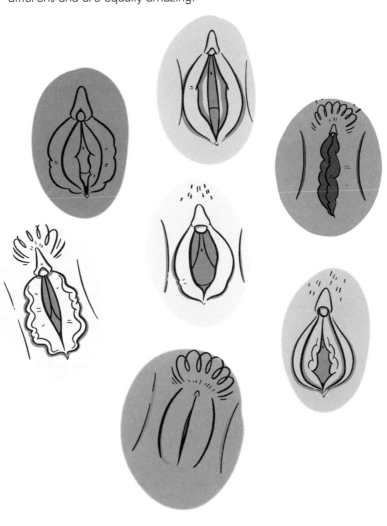

OK, back to body hair . . . The fact is, we all have hair all over our bodies from the moment we're born, but until puberty it tends to be very fair and hard to see. Pubic hair is much thicker and so the tendency can be to want to cover it up or to feel confused about how to deal with it. You might also notice that the hair on your legs starts to get thicker during puberty too. More recently, some people have started to embrace body hair and to just leave it to grow naturally, which is great as there's no medical or hygiene reason to get rid of body hair.

If you do want to remove some of your body hair that's OK too, but it can be difficult and overwhelming knowing which method to choose, so let me break down the options for you . . .

Shaving

It can be really tempting to pick up a razor in the first instance – they're easy, cheap and accessible, and the chances are someone else in your house will already have one. But before you pick a razor up, ask a parent, caregiver or trusted older sibling to help you the first time so you avoid cutting yourself – and follow this step by step guide . . .

1. Lather up the area you want to shave with soap or shaving foam to avoid getting a rash

2. Shave in the direction that the hair grows

3. You might need to go over the same area a few times to get all the hairs

4. Rinse off any residual soap and dry your skin

5. Apply a moisturiser to sooth your skin and avoid a rash

Remember to never shave the hairs on your face, as shaving can make the hairs look thicker and darker when they grow back because they'll be blunt and stubbly. This can also be a very good reason to leave starting to shave your body hair till as late as possible, as once you start, you'll have to do it regularly for upkeep.

Hair removal creams

Creams work by dissolving the hair to below the skin's surface and sometimes all the way to the root. The advantage of creams is that there is no danger of cutting yourself and you can get to the tricky places like your armpits that are awkward to reach with a razor. They can be messy though, and you have to be careful to apply the cream correctly. They also have quite a strong smell, but you can get perfumed versions. Always do a patch test before using a cream for the first time to check you aren't allergic.

Waxing

Waxing removes the hair from the root but home waxing can be painful and very messy, and you can get yourself into a very sticky situation! So I recommend you get a parent to help or go to a waxing salon. Because waxing removes the hair from the root, it does stop some of it from growing back, and the hair that does return gradually grows back finer over time. A quick word of warning though: curly and afro hair can get stuck when growing back and this can cause 'ingrown hairs' with spots and inflammation. If this happens to you, wear loose-fitting clothes to avoid friction, cleanse the skin with fragrance-free soap or cleanser and apply a mild gel like aloe vera or tea tree oil to soothe the skin. And don't panic! Most inflammation will fade within a couple of days.

TIPS

FOR WAXING

- Exfoliate the skin beforehand
- Apply talcum powder to the skin to absorb any moisture
- Check the temperature of the wax before applying so you don't burn yourself
- Support the skin to hold the area taut
- Pull the strip off quickly in the opposite direction to hair growth
- Moisturise your skin afterwards

Epilator

My mum used to get her legs and armpits waxed and she always told me to never shave because I have dark hair and it would make it appear to grow back thicker. Waxing makes your hair grow back finer but back then we couldn't afford this option, so we bought an epilator for £15 from an advert in the paper. An epilator is a little handheld device that plucks out unwanted hair from the root. My auntie came round and she and my mum pretty much pinned me down (with my permission!) while they removed my leg and armpit hair. I'm really grateful they did though, because I used the epilator for the first two years and now my leg hair is really fine. You can buy an epilator from big chemists and though they are more expensive than razors (you might want to ask for one for your birthday), they will last much longer so might work out cheaper in the long run.

FOR EPILATING

- Exfoliate the skin before
- Take a warm shower before to open the pores
- Keep the skin taut
- Start on a less sensitive area such as the lower leg
- Take breaks if the pain gets too intense

Laser

Laser hair removal is becoming more and more popular because it results in more long-lasting hair removal. I recommend laser treatment to patients if they're having lots of difficulties with other methods. The downside is that laser hair removal is expensive in the short term (but it may save money in the long run) and usually only available to people over fourteen. I have had laser treatment and the hairs in my armpits are gone for ever. It wasn't previously available for dark skinned people because the laser works by spotting the difference in pigment between the hair and skin. But thankfully the technology has moved on so it can now be effective for all skin tones.

Body odour

Eww – what is that smell? Well, it could be you or it could be me, because I'm sorry to break it to you, we all smell. And when you go through puberty, you might notice that those areas where you've started growing hair might start to smell differently to how they did before. This can be stressful but it's nothing to worry about. Your skin has two types of sweat glands: eccrine and apocrine. Eccrine glands occur over most of your body and the sweat they produce doesn't smell, it's mostly to help us cool down. Apocrine glands are located mostly in the armpits and pubic area, and they don't become active until puberty. The sweat from apocrine glands contains oils which provide food for bacteria and that's what causes the smell.

Here are some simple steps you can take to stop body odour.

Washing

Take a shower or wash your armpits and pubic area using soap and a flannel or sponge at least once every day to help keep body odour at bay. It works because you are washing away the bacteria on your skin before they can start to produce a bad smell.

Deodorant

A deodorant doesn't stop you from sweating – it usually has a nice smell which aims to overpower or mask the smell of body odour.

Antiperspirant

An antiperspirant contains chemicals (usually aluminium based) that reduce or stop the sweating. It works anywhere you tend to sweat, but should never be applied to the nose, eyes, mouth or genitals. Most deodorants and antiperspirants are effective for 24 hours so you only need to apply them once a day, after washing, on clean dry skin.

There's no point going to all the trouble of washing and wearing deodorant if the clothes you wear are dirty and smell of sweat, so make sure you wear fresh clothes every day, and this especially applies to your underwear.

See your GP

If your sweating is very excessive and it's really affecting you, I recommend you ask your parent or caregiver to help you book an appointment with your GP.

Shhhh, overshare moment . . .

I'm sitting in the gym right now, writing this section before I do a class. And I just had a little sniff of my right armpit . . . Not smelling fresh! I didn't shower this morning as I was coming straight to the gym and will shower after my class. I didn't use an antiperspirant either, as my routine is to put that on after my shower! So I'm a bit stinky! It's not the end of the world, and we all forget sometimes, but I will be trying to keep to my own space in the fitness class!

Breasts

OK, so we've conquered the spot volcanoes that have erupted on our face, we've tamed the mischievous hair that keeps popping up in unexpected places and we've got our body odour under control, but what about our breasts that seem to have taken on a life of their own? Another physical change you will experience in puberty is your breasts developing and growing bigger. Why is this happening? Well, biologically, your body is basically adapting so that it is capable of feeding any babies you might have in the future.

The first change you will notice are 'breast buds', which are hard, firm lumps beneath your nipples. This usually happens on one side first so please don't worry if this is the case – the other side will catch up soon.

Over time you will start to notice breast tissue developing. As with everything in puberty, people develop breast tissue at different

times so don't worry if your friends need to wear a bra before you do. It's common to feel self-conscious about body changes like these and you might feel that you don't want others to see. That's perfectly OK; it takes time getting used to body changes and I recommend you take your time getting to know your new breasts. One way to do this is to get into the practice of checking your boobs once a month for any changes or bumps. This is a great habit to get into as the more familiar you are with your breasts from a young age, the easier you will find it to check your breasts throughout your life to make sure they are healthy.

Breasts come in all different shapes and sizes, and with different nipple types – some are dark, some are light, some protrude, some are inverted. It doesn't matter what they look like, your breasts are your friends and everyone's are different, unique and beautiful.

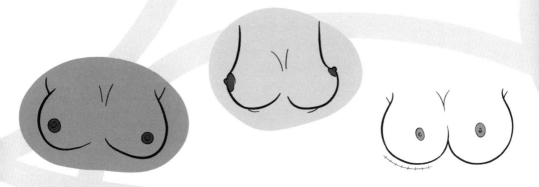

MYTH BUSTER

There's nothing you can do to speed up or slow down your breast development — and it's not true that creams, or sleeping on your front, or certain exercises can make a difference to how they grow.

I was super self-conscious about my body once I got breasts and pubic hair, to the point where I wouldn't even let my mum see me naked any more. Something that completely changed that for me was when I went to university and started playing rugby. I knew that after my first competitive game we were all going to shower together. I had no idea how this was going to go down, and I wondered if people would wear their swimsuits to shower in, so I took my bikini just in case. After the game we were all covered in mud, and everyone just stripped off and got in the shower. I saw all kinds of different women with different kinds of bodies that day. Some had pubic hair, some had none. Some had bigger, droopier breasts than mine and some had flatter chests. But the great thing was, no one cared! We'd won the game and we were all singing songs and having a great time, and I couldn't believe I'd had such a problem with being seen naked before. It was such an empowering moment.

And of course, since becoming a GP, I've really seen how different we all are physically. If I could go back and speak to my younger self, I'd tell her . . .

'No one's going to JUDGE YOU and nobody really CARES because they're too busy STRESSING ABOUT THEMSELVES, so STOP WORRYING!'

CHALLENGE

If you've been feeling self-conscious about your changing body, I challenge you to be brave enough to get changed with confidence just one time in the swimming pool or PE changing rooms. Hopefully you'll have the same light bulb moment and surge of body confidence I did that day after rugby.

Buying your first bra

Once your breasts start to grow, wearing a bra or crop top will bring you comfort and support. Buying your first bra is a momentous occasion but it can also feel overwhelming, especially when it comes to knowing which size and style you ought to get. The good news is there are plenty of bra size calculators online – all you'll need is a measuring tape and possibly a calculator, depending on your maths skills!

It's totally understandable if you feel awkward about broaching the subject with your parents or carers but I'm sure they will be expecting it. You could say that you're starting to feel some discomfort or sensitivity in your chest area or tell them that your friends are all beginning to wear starter bras.

Crop tops are the best option at first, when your nipples start to protrude. Once the breasts start to develop, you can move up to a soft-cup starter bra, or teen bra. These are designed for comfort and coverage and tend to be made of stretchable cotton. Sports bras offer more support and are great for PE lessons if you're finding that running or jumping about is causing discomfort.

Weight gain

During puberty, it is perfectly normal to put on weight. One obvious reason for this is that you are growing taller, and another is the increase in fatty tissue all over the body. This is your body biologically preparing itself so that one day it could possibly bear children. In fact, a certain amount of fat in the body is necessary for you to start and keep having regular menstrual cycles. Your hips will likely get wider and, due to the hormones, your body will change shape and get curvier. So please don't worry if you start putting on weight around your breasts, hips, thighs and bottom – it's all part of your body transforming into an adult, which is a beautiful thing.

But it's important to note that some people don't put on much weight during puberty. I was like a beanpole until I reached eighteen! So much is outside of our control and based on our genetics – characteristics we inherit from our parents and ancestors. You can be really sporty, active and eat healthily and still put on weight during puberty – that is normal. And you may have friends who don't eat as healthily as you or who do little exercise and stay thin because this is mostly determined by their genetics.

The most important thing to remember is that body health is *not* determined solely by body size. Someone who appears very slim but eats a lot of junk food, smokes, doesn't exercise and doesn't get enough sleep will be less healthy overall than someone who has a larger body, eats a nutritious diet, doesn't smoke, does a lot of walking and gets plenty of sleep. Health is about how you live in all areas of your life.

Many of us struggle to accept the body that we have, whatever it is like. There will be girls who wish they had more curves and bigger boobs, there will be girls who wish they had more muscle, and some will wish they were just smaller.

I was chatting recently with my friend Sarah, who is the founder and director of an organisation that supports people living with obesity, and she told me that if she could go back and speak to her teenage self, she would say, 'Embrace who you are. Everyone comes in different shapes and sizes, we are never all going to look the same,

and that is the beauty of diversity. I wish I had just embraced my boobs and hips, loved my curves and not then spent the next 25 years trying to change my body shape, through trying every diet going and punishing myself in the gym. Who knows, if I had just embraced who I was and not dieted for ever, I might not actually be living with obesity right now, but just living a happy, healthy, curvy size 14 life!'

I know that all of the changes that happen to your body during puberty are a lot to take in, but I hope this chapter has prepared you and made you see that they are also a truly wonderful thing.

CHAPTER 2

PERIODS

One major physical change you will experience during puberty – so major it deserves its very own chapter – is starting your menstrual cycle, aka your periods.

You might have heard a lot about this before from family, friends or on telly, or it might be completely new to you. But in a nutshell, a period is when a small amount of blood and tissue from the lining of the uterus comes out of your vagina for a few days roughly once a month. This blood and tissue tends to be red to dark red in colour, although it can sometimes look black or brown, and seeing some clots is normal too.

Periods

Before you start your periods, the thought of blood coming from your vagina every month can feel kind of scary, so it's important to remember that this is a normal part of life for most girls and women around the world – and always has been.

When periods first start, they can be erratic, irregular and unpredictable. Most people settle into what will become their menstrual cycle after the first year. We are all different, so while some girls have a period every 28 days, a normal cycle length is anywhere between 21 and 40 days. The period itself normally lasts between 2 and 8 days.

I'll talk a bit later in this chapter about how to manage problem periods, but first let's get to grips with what exactly is happening in normal periods. The menstrual cycle can be broken down into four phases, and each part comes with its own side effects and superpowers – yes, you read that last one right!

Remember what I said in the last chapter about knowledge being power? Well, once you know exactly what your body is going through at any given time, you can start to use your cycle to your advantage.

In short, I'm going to teach you how to hack your hormones! There are many different hormones that go up and down throughout the cycle, but to avoid getting too complicated I'll focus mostly on how oestrogen and progesterone hormones change.

So let's start by breaking down the menstrual cycle . . .

The four phases of the menstrual cycle

2. Follicular phase

3. Luteal phase

4. Premenstrual phase

1. Menstrual phase

1. Menstrual phase (around days 1-8)

The first phase of the menstrual cycle is when we menstruate. This is when the lining of the uterus is shed, along with some blood, and you have your period. It usually lasts between 2 and 8 days and you may, but not always, experience some period pain.

Side effects... During this time, we tend to feel a bit delicate. The brain is more susceptible to pain, so our pain threshold is lower. Hormone levels are low and this can make us feel emotional or low in mood. Understanding the reasons for the emotional changes and knowing they won't last can be helpful.

Superpowers... This first phase is a bit like winter and it's a good time for our brain to do focused thinking. It's actually a great time for planning, study and getting schoolwork done. Physically, you may want to slow down, rest and be gentle with yourself, but some exercise is good as it can make you feel more energised and give your mood a boost.

2. Follicular phase (around days 8-14)

The follicular phase comes next. This is when several eggs mature inside follicles, which are like sacs, within the ovary. We think of it as the time after menstruation until ovulation (but strictly speaking it actually includes the menstruation phase too).

Side effects ... The hormone oestrogen is high at this time, and it makes us feel great. We are likely to feel at our best. Our pain threshold is higher and psychologically we have a boost of drive and confidence.

Superpowers ... This phase can feel like spring and re-emerging from hibernation. It's a great time to try out new sports or activities, meet new people and enjoy social events (are you scheduling a birthday party?). For the athletes out there this is the best time of the month to go for your personal best.

3. Luteal phase (around days 15-21)

This phase starts with ovulation, which is when the egg is released from the biggest follicle. It travels from the ovary, down the fallopian tube, to the uterus. Once in the uterus, it will dissolve after about 24–28 hours if not fertilised by sperm.

Side effects ... Oestrogen levels start to dip and another hormone called progesterone rises. You're likely to still feel bright and energised and you may have an increased appetite. Towards the end of this phase, memory can be less focused.

Superpowers... This phase of the cycle is like summertime. It's a great time to go out and have fun. A brilliant time for being active, going on long hikes or bike rides or playing loads of sport. Towards the end you might benefit from starting to wind down.

4. Premenstrual phase (around days 22-28)

If a pregnancy has not occurred, you then enter the fourth phase of the menstrual cycle, which is the premenstrual phase.

Side effects... Oestrogen and progesterone levels both drop quite rapidly in this phase, making you more likely to feel the typical symptoms of premenstrual syndrome (PMS) – which include headaches, bloating, breast pain, anxiety, anger and low mood. Energy levels can dip and you may find it more difficult to concentrate for long periods of time.

Superpowers... This phase of the cycle is like autumn, and everything can start to feel a bit dull and lifeless. Do schoolwork in shorter bursts and give yourself smaller tasks, rather than working at a hundred per cent effort all day. This is the time of the month to make self-care your superpower. Schedule in time for reading, long baths or walks in nature – whatever works for you. You can still do whatever sport or exercise you wish and it's also a great time for trying more restorative forms of exercise like yoga or Pilates.

Hormone hacking

Now we've broken down the menstrual cycle into these phases, it becomes easier to see how you can hack your hormones and make your cycle work for you. Hormone hacking isn't about changing your hormone levels, it's more about planning your month around your cycle so you can get the best out of each phase. I totally understand that there are some aspects of life you can't control, for example having to go to school during phase four when you might really prefer a duvet day at home. But you can still prioritise self-care during this time, just as you can prioritise going out and having fun in phases two and three!

Dr Zoe's Prescription

Keep a diary of your cycle

The most important thing to recognise is that we are all unique, so keeping a diary to log how you feel and function at different times in your cycle can be really helpful. After a few months you may start to see a pattern. Once you know the science of yourself, you can start planning your diary according to your superpowers at that specific time in the cycle.

Sanitary products

Deciding which sanitary products to use can be even more daunting than trying to pick which bra to start with – there's so much to choose from. Let me break it down for you to hopefully make it a little easier . . .

Sanitary towels (or pads)

A sanitary towel is a pad worn inside your underwear to absorb menstrual blood. Pads range in size according to how heavy or light your bleed is. And you can get special pads to wear while you sleep at night. Lots of girls find these the easiest to use when they first start their periods. Especially ones with wings (not for flying, unfortunately) that help keep the pad in place!

Tampons

Tampons also absorb menstrual blood but they do it inside your body rather than outside. Tampons are a plug of soft material that you insert into the vagina and they have a little string at the bottom so you can easily pull them back out. They come in different sizes and absorbencies. When you first start your periods, the thought of inserting a tampon can be a little scary so most people start with pads and move on to tampons when – and if – they feel ready. The advantage of tampons is that they make sport easier as they're worn inside and less visible. It's important to remember that tampons need to be changed regularly – every three to five hours – to avoid toxic shock syndrome (TSS), which is caused by the growth of bad bacteria. TSS can also be caused by using a higher absorbency tampon than you need, so if your tampon isn't saturated after three to five hours, switch to a lower absorbency.

Menstrual cups

Menstrual cups are inserted into the vagina just like a tampon, but instead of absorbing the blood they collect it. The great thing about them is that they're reusable. When they're full you simply take them out, give them a wash and pop them back in. This isn't just great for the environment – it's great if you don't have much money for sanitary products too.

MYTH BUSTER

You're going on a beach holiday or have a swimming lesson booked and disaster strikes – you get your period! Surely you can't go swimming when you have your monthly bleed, can you? Actually, yes, you can. When you're swimming, the water pressure reduces the flow of menstrual blood from the vagina, but it's important to note that as soon as you come out of the water that pressure will change, so it's best to wear a tampon or menstrual cup.

Period pants

Period pants are just like normal pants but they have a built-in, super absorbant and leak-resistant lining, meaning you don't need to use a tampon or sanitary towel. They do cost a lot more than regular pants but they're washable and reusable, so when you think of how much money you'll be saving on tampons or sanitary pads they seem a lot more reasonable. You can get period swimwear too.

Panty liners

Panty liners are basically a sanitary towel's super-thin sister and they're great for the days when your periods are light. They're also great for vaginal discharge.

Shhhh, overshare moment . . .

Because I started my periods a bit later than most of my friends, I was desperate to start and was very inquisitive about tampons in particular. I used to raid my mum's box of Tampax whenever I was in the loo and read the information leaflet and obsessively study the picture that showed how to insert the tampon. I tried it out a few times too but had no luck. Once my periods started, I soon wished they'd go away again, and using tampons got instantly much easier and soon wasn't novel at all!

I know sanitary protection can be overwhelming when you first start your periods but if it's any consolation, things are so much better than they used to be in the olden days, when women would have to put a piece of sheepskin or moss in their knickers to absorb the blood!

Vaginal discharge

Vaginal discharge might sound a little worrying but it is perfectly normal. It is basically a fluid/mucus that keeps the vagina clean, lubricated and free from infection. The amount of discharge you get tends to vary according to the time of the month, and during ovulation it is usually clear and more slippery – a bit like raw egg white.

Signs of healthy discharge are . . .
- No strong smell
- Clear or white in colour
- Thick and sticky or wet in consistency

You only need to worry about your discharge if you experience any of the following . . .
- Strong, pungent odour
- White and lumpy like cottage cheese
- It comes with pelvic pain and/or bleeding
- You feel itchy or sore
- Dark yellow, green, brown or bloody discharge

If you experience any of these, you should see your doctor as it could be a sign of infection.

Keeping your Vagina clean

You can use just plain water or a mild unscented soap to wash your vulva (the external genitals), but there is no need to wash your vagina (the inside part of your genitals) as it is so clever it cleans itself. Disturbing the vagina's natural environment by douching (pushing water into the vagina) or using scented soap can lead to infection or irritation.

Period poverty

According to a recent study, one in ten girls in the UK can't afford to buy sanitary products, which can lead to them missing school or feeling really uncomfortable in lessons. Charities are now providing free sanitary products in schools and you can also get free sanitary products from your local food bank. Reusable products like period pants and menstrual cups are also great money-savers over the long term. See the back of this book for resources on period poverty and where you can find free period products.

When periods go wrong

Sometimes periods can be painful, heavy or irregular, but all of these can be treated and managed. If you're missing school, not participating in sports or not staying over at friends' houses because of your periods, there's no need to suffer in silence. If this is something you're worried about, ask a parent, caregiver or trusted adult to contact your GP, or talk to your school nurse about it. And you can also visit your GP on your own if you wish to do so.

Heavy periods

You might have heard people use the word 'flow' to describe their periods. This basically means how heavy, or light, their bleed is. It might sometimes feel like a lot more but the average woman loses six to eight teaspoonfuls of blood every month. A person's periods can vary in terms of flow over the years and sometimes it can be classed as heavy. The medical term for this, if you really want to impress your doctor, is **menorrhagia** (pronounced meh-nuh-ray-jee-uh). Have a read of the questions below. If you answer yes to two or more, or if the heavy bleeding is stopping you from enjoying things, then it's worth discussing with your GP.

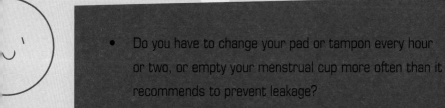

- Do you have to change your pad or tampon every hour or two, or empty your menstrual cup more often than it recommends to prevent leakage?

- Do you need to use two types of sanitary product, such as a pad and a tampon, a pad and a menstrual cup, or two pads together, to prevent leaks?

- Do you often bleed through to your clothes or bedding during your period?

- Do you usually pass large blood clots?

- Do you regularly take time off school or activities because of your heavy periods?

- Do you often have to get up in the night to change your tampon or pad, or empty your menstrual cup?

- Do you frequently avoid exercising during your period because you're worried about potential leakage?

- Do you feel excessively tired or short of breath?

If you have heavy periods and you often feel excessively tired or short of breath, it could be a sign of iron deficiency anaemia caused by blood loss during your period. See your GP for a simple blood test, which will confirm if you're anaemic. You should also see your GP if you experience bleeding between your periods.

A hot water bottle or heat pad

Gentle, low-impact exercise, like swimming or walking

Dark chocolate — seriously, it has been known to relax muscles and ease cramps!

Ginger or camomile tea

Taking a warm bath or shower

Painful periods

The medical name for this is **dysmenorrhea** (pronounced di-smeh-nuh-ree-uh). Period pains are common, especially on the first and second day of a period. They are caused by the muscles in the uterus contracting and tend to be crampy, and they can be felt in the lower tummy, back and legs. Painkillers such as paracetamol and ibuprofen can help a lot and work best if taken before the pain gets bad. So it's best to take them as soon as you feel the first cramp and continue taking them regularly for as long as you are affected by the pain. If you're logging and tracking your menstrual cycle, then you may know exactly when the pain will come and you can even get ahead of it by taking pain relief beforehand. If that is not working and the pain is still so bad that it is stopping you from doing the things you want, it's time to see your GP, who can discuss other solutions. On the previous page are some other tips for easing period pain.

Irregular periods

I mentioned earlier that cycle length can vary from person to person, and a cycle length between 21 and 40 days is deemed normal. Irregular periods are when the length between each period keeps changing, or when periods keep being missed. It's very common for periods to be irregular at the start, during puberty, for the first year or two, but after that it should be discussed with a doctor. There are many possible causes, such as extreme weight loss or weight gain, excessive exercise or stress, some types of contraception and also some medical conditions – such as polycystic ovary syndrome (PCOS) or a problem with your thyroid.

What about the boys?

So, you might be thinking that it's only girls who are invited to the puberty party – but don't worry, boys experience dramatic changes during this time too.

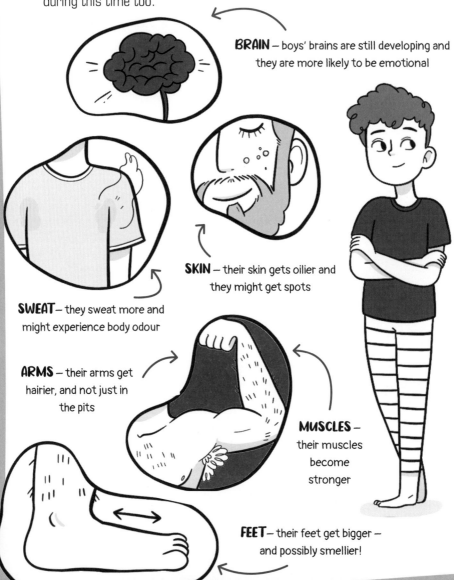

BRAIN – boys' brains are still developing and they are more likely to be emotional

SKIN – their skin gets oilier and they might get spots

SWEAT – they sweat more and might experience body odour

ARMS – their arms get hairier, and not just in the pits

MUSCLES – their muscles become stronger

FEET – their feet get bigger – and possibly smellier!

WET DREAMS – they sometimes ejaculate in their sleep after having a dream of a sexual nature

HAIR – they get body hair and hair on their face

VOICE – due to increased testosterone their voice 'breaks', which basically means it gets deeper

CHEST – their nipples might become sensitive and swollen

BODY – their chest and shoulders get broader

LEGS – their legs get longer and hairier

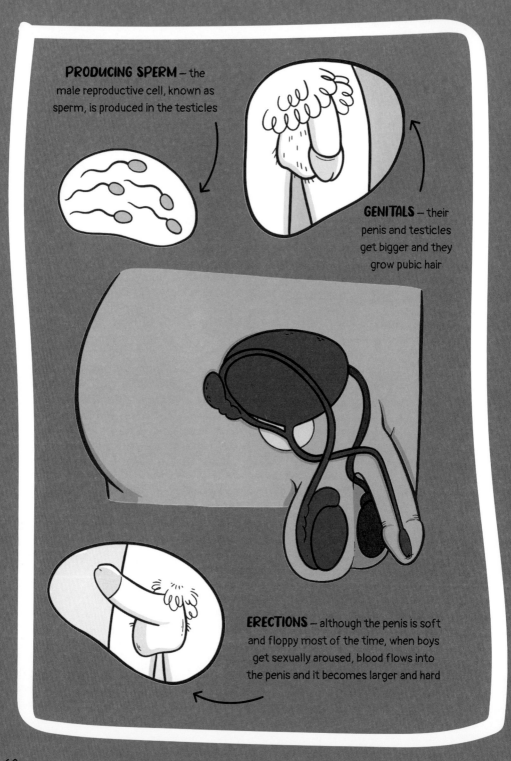

PRODUCING SPERM – the male reproductive cell, known as sperm, is produced in the testicles

GENITALS – their penis and testicles get bigger and they grow pubic hair

ERECTIONS – although the penis is soft and floppy most of the time, when boys get sexually aroused, blood flows into the penis and it becomes larger and hard

CHAPTER 3

WONDERFUL YOU AND GROWING YOUR CONFIDENCE

Well, after all of those physical changes you're likely to experience in puberty, it's hardly surprising if you end up feeling like your emotions are all over the place. Periods, spots, PMS, vaginal discharge – coupled with school, homework, friends and family – it's a lot! But puberty doesn't have to be a hormonal horror story, I promise. Before we dive into this pool of emotions, here are some of my favourite tips for when your mood dips . . .

Managing your emotions

Acceptance

Firstly, there are no 'bad' feelings. You're allowed to feel sad or grumpy or angry at times, and actually, I've found that when you accept these so-called negative feelings, they leave a whole lot quicker than when you fight them. As the saying goes, what you resist persists. So the next time you're feeling down, just say to yourself, 'I'm feeling down today, and that's OK.'

Distraction

Distraction can be another great way to lift yourself out of a funk. Binge on a fave TV series, lose yourself in a video game or put on some music and dance round your bedroom. Go for a walk. All can be great ways of taking your mind off things.

Write it out

Write your feelings on to the page. Journaling can be a great way of alleviating the pressure. And if you're feeling cross or sad about something someone's done to you, why not write them a letter that you'll never send but just as a way of getting things off your chest.

Breathe yourself calm

A really quick and simple way of calming your emotions is through your breathing. Focus on breathing slowly and deeply, in through the nose and out through the mouth. I guarantee that after a minute of this you'll be feeling calmer.

In chapter 7 you'll find a breathing exercise that you can use to help you relax.

Growing your confidence

I hope you're someone who feels confident in yourself and excited about growing up. But from time to time, we can all lack self-belief or compare ourselves to others. Before the age of eight there's little difference between boys and girls when it comes to confidence levels. But as soon as girls reach puberty, studies show their confidence levels start to fall, whereas boys' stay the same. But things don't have to be that way. So in this chapter I'm going to share my tips for staying self-assured and confident from puberty all the way to adulthood.

As I mentioned earlier, I was a very shy child, due in part to my asthma and being the only non-white child in my class at primary school. My nervousness continued into my teenage years, which made me prone to peer pressure. I had a real desire to be liked, accepted and popular so I made some decisions that I now really regret.

One example of this was having my afro hair chemically straightened. I did this because I wanted to fit in and I hated it if anyone commented on my hair. The irony is, as an adult I love my afro hair – it's a major part of my identity and now that I'm on TV it makes me instantly recognisable, which I love.

So here are my tips for growing your confidence . . .

Reframe your differences

My mum really helped me become proud of my differences instead of embarrassed by them. Whenever we saw someone with a perm, which was really popular when I was growing up in the 1980s, she'd say, 'Look at all the people spending a fortune to get curly hair and you have it naturally.'

Another thing that was popular in the 1980s was having a sunbed in your bedroom. At night you'd see the distinctive glow shining from the windows. Mum would always point them out, telling me that these people were spending loads of money and risking their health to get browner, so if anyone was mean about my skin colour it was just because they were jealous.

Think about something that makes you different and self-conscious as a result. How could you reframe it as something positive? How could you be proud of who you are and what makes you different? Try writing a list of ideas for inspiration.

Use body language

A few years ago I was on a sports entertainment show called *Gladiators*, where contestants had to compete in physical events against a cast of Gladiators. I was one of the Gladiators, named Amazon. As a Gladiator I was supposed to be super fit and strong. But I experienced a huge crisis of confidence in one of the events, due to my fear of heights. The event was called the Pyramid and I had to stand right at the very top of this huge pyramid on a platform. If this wasn't bad enough, the platform had gaps in the floor so I could see right through to the ground, oh so far below. I was terrified. But while the contestants on the show were allowed to look scared, as one of the Gladiators, I most definitely wasn't.

As I was standing there desperately trying not to be sick or tremble, the stage director called through my earpiece: 'Amazon, pose two to camera five!' All of us Gladiators had different choreographed poses to make us look strong and brave. Pose two involved putting one hand in the air and the other on my hips like a statue and staring confidently into the camera. As I did the pose the strangest thing happened – by acting confident I started to *feel* it and my fear of heights faded!

Dr Zoe's Prescription

Pull a power pose

Give yourself a gladiator name and pull a power pose of your own. Feet apart, hands on hips, head up, chest out! How does it make you feel? Practise this every day for a week, then the next time you need to be brave, remember your gladiator name and slightly shift towards your pose, as a reminder that you've got this! Research has shown that the way we approach the world with our physical bodies can change the way we think and feel.

The magic of mantras

If a friend confided in you that she was feeling a little anxious about an upcoming exam, would you reply, 'I'm not surprised, you're bound to fail'? Or if a loved one told you that she was worried she didn't look good, would you smirk and say, 'You're right, that colour definitely doesn't suit you, and look at the state of your hair'?

I really hope you answered an instant 'no' to those questions! You may not have spoken to a friend or loved one like that but it's really common for girls, and women, to speak to themselves that way on a regular basis.

We all have an inner critic, a mean little voice in our head that likes to tell us we aren't good enough, clever enough or pretty enough, and if we don't do something to counter that voice it can run the show and literally steal our happiness and opportunities. One of the best ways of drowning out your inner critic is through using mantras.

A mantra is a positive statement that you repeat over and over, to reinforce the meaning of the words. My favourite mantra is: **Yes, I can!** My mum taught it to me when I was young and lacked confidence. At that time in life I always used to say, *'No, I can't.'* It wasn't just Mum who helped me by using this mantra. I used to get so nervous running the 200 metres in athletics for my school that I'd be shaking like a leaf on the start line and saying, 'No, I can't do this,' over and over in my head. Knowing this, my PE teacher used to stand by me booming, **'Yes, you can!'** in her broad Scottish accent!

Here are some positive mantras for you to try . . .

I have got what it takes

YES, I CAN

I AM ENOUGH

I'm beautiful inside and out

Once you've chosen your mantra or mantras, keep them somewhere you'll be reminded of them. For example, you could write them on a Post-it and stick it on your mirror or build it into your screensavers.

Whenever you feel your confidence dip, say your mantra in your head at least ten times.

Tame your inner troll

It can also help to see your negative inner voice as a funny little troll. The troll doesn't mean to hurt you; it's actually trying to keep you safe by telling you not to take a risk that might leave you embarrassed or upset. But the problem is, it's way too over-sensitive!

Try drawing your inner troll (or download a funny picture of a troll) and give it a name. The next time it tries to tell you that you aren't good enough, imagine saying, 'Thanks but no thanks.' Be kind and gentle with your troll but remind it that you are the boss and you are good enough, then imagine yourself zipping up its mouth!

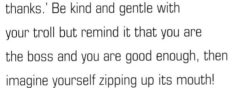

Physical exercise, let's get moving

When I was young and suffering from severe asthma, my doctor gave me what is known as a social prescription and recommended that I take up physical exercise. He felt that exercise would help my asthma because it would help my lungs work better, but it would also help me grow my confidence.

The first sport I ever had lessons in was dance, and it ended up massively changing me and my life for the better. I made lots of new friends through dance and became very competitive. This competitive spirit spilled over into other areas of my life, like the classroom. I loved feeling further ahead of my classmates and actually got quite annoyed if someone did better than me in a test, especially if it was a boy. This competitiveness in the classroom, and the motivation that came with it, definitely made a huge difference to my grades in school.

When my mum could no longer afford to send me to dance class, I took the opportunity to do every sport I could in school, such as running, hockey and netball, and from the age of fourteen I never needed to use an inhaler again. Physical exercise helped me overcome my asthma, gave me confidence and made me competitive – the best exchange ever!

Is there a sport that you've been wanting to try? Or a school team you'd like to try out for? Whatever it is, I say go for it! And if it's challenging at first, that's all part of it, so stick with it!

Reframe your fear as excitement

If you ever ask someone competing in extreme sports like BMX racing or bobsledding how they feel right before competing, they'll tell you that they aren't afraid, they're excited. Interestingly, our bodies have the exact same physical responses when we're afraid or excited, which include . . .

- High levels of stress hormone
- Dry mouth
- Tunnel vision
- Feeling a bit shaky

You'd probably describe the feelings you get on a rollercoaster as excitement, but if you experienced them before giving a presentation to your whole class, you'd call them nerves.

The next time you're feeling nervous, try telling yourself you're excited. It's amazing what a difference this shift in mindset can make.

Body image

Our bodies are amazing. They do so much for us and carry us through life, so it's a real shame when they become a reason for us losing confidence. But during puberty when your body is changing so much, it can be hard adjusting and you can end up feeling really self-conscious about the curves that are suddenly starting to appear in random places, not to mention the hair and the spots.

We also live in a culture that's obsessed with appearance, so it can be really hard to stay immune to this. You probably know this but so many of the images you see around you in adverts, in magazines and online have been manipulated, airbrushed and filtered so you can't see all the things that every human body has – like stretch marks and spots and cellulite in all sorts of places. This makes us think that there is something wrong with our bodies but there isn't at all. In fact, a lot of the images we see around us would be impossible to achieve in real life! As a result, a lot of teen girls and women end up using filters on their social media photos, which mask these so-called blemishes, and it can make us feel ashamed of our true selves.

A great way to counteract everyone's obsession with appearance is to focus on how amazing our bodies are instead. Sport and exercise can play a great role here. When you are able to run a certain distance or jump a certain height, it helps you appreciate your body for what it can do rather than how it can look.

Rugby really helped me become more positive about my body and less obsessed with how I looked. As soon as I was in the changing room showers with all those amazing women and their vastly different bodies – complete with stretch marks, cellulite, spots and pubic hair – I recognised that I was in awe of those real women because of what their bodies could *do* on the field, much more than the fake images of women who looked a certain way in magazines.

Here are some fun facts about your body to help you appreciate it more . . .

- Every second your body produces 25 million new cells

- There are around 60,000 miles of blood vessels in your body – enough to go around the world twice!

- There are 22 different bones in your skull

- You have between about 2 million and 5 million sweat glands on your body

- Humans are one of the best creatures in the world at long-distance running

- Weight for weight, your bones are stronger than steel

- When you sneeze, the air comes out of your body at a speed of up to 93 miles per hour!

- Your body is made of stardust – it really is, ask your science teacher!

Curate your social media feeds

You have to be over thirteen to join most social media platforms and it's important to consult your parent or caregiver before signing up, but when you are old enough to join, here are my tips for protecting your confidence and mental health while online. And remember, be cyber-safe at all times and never share your personal details with someone you don't know.

If you're looking at content online that makes you feel bad about yourself and chips away at your confidence, I highly recommend curating (that means carefully selecting) who you follow. The next time you're scrolling, take a mental note of how different content makes you feel. If someone's content makes you feel bad, I'd adopt the 'three strikes and you're out' rule. In other words, if they've made you feel bad three or more times, unfollow them or hide their posts from your feed. You're too wonderful and precious to feel bad about something that frankly has nothing to do with you.

Another thing I'd recommend is to limit the time you spend on social media and follow people who make you feel good or make you laugh.

And remember that most, if not all, of the images you're seeing will be filtered in some way, so it's not reality. You can think of someone's Instagram feed as a highlights reel, showing you the best single moment of the day, and not all the crap that goes on in life too. In fact, often it's not even a genuine moment in their day, its usually something that has been set up just for 'the gram', so take it all with a large pinch of salt.

If you feel the pressure to use Facetune or filters on your own posts, things can get really tricky. You're almost creating a fictional person who doesn't exist and you're setting yourself up to fail. Even if you do get positive comments, they're for the filtered you, not the real you.

Instead, I challenge you to celebrate your uniqueness and be proud of who you are, warts and all.

Dr Zoe's Prescription

Five Likes

Stand in front of the mirror and list five things you really like about yourself – or you could do this exercise with a friend and list five things you like about yourselves and each other. Own your uniqueness instead of airbrushing it away.

There's no doubt that puberty can be a tricky time emotionally and sometimes your confidence will be shaken, but hopefully the tips and tools in this chapter will help you come back to a place of balance.

Any time you feel yourself having a wobble, come back to these techniques and know that it will pass. At the end of the day it's all a part of you growing up and becoming your own unique and wonderful self, and this should be celebrated.

CHAPTER 4

KEEPING HEALTHY

Now, you might be someone who absolutely loves sport, is part of every school team and wishes they could do PE all day, every day. Or you might absolutely dread that time of the week when you have to get into your sports gear and do some exercise. Your feelings might change over time too. When you're going through puberty, it's not uncommon to fall out of love with a sport you once loved, or to suddenly feel much more self-conscious than you ever did before. You're not alone. Studies show that between the ages of eleven and fifteen, girls' fitness levels drop quite dramatically.

I've visited schools and spoken to girls about this, trying to find out why they no longer want to take part in sport or fitness, and a big reason is down to appearance. They don't want to mess up their hair and make-up and they don't want boys to see them being physically active – reasons that don't affect the boys.

But I see fitness as my medicine and it keeps me healthy physically and mentally. Exercise has also led to me making lifelong friends with my teammates. So in this chapter, we're not going to let ourselves (or the boys) stop us from staying fit and healthy, feeling good and doing what we love. Exercise can be fun and here's how . . .

Keep trying different things

When I was at school, I loved dancing as a team or with a partner and I also did netball, hockey, cross country and football. But it wasn't until university that I found my true sporting passion – rugby.

So don't be afraid to keep trying different sports and physical activities – you never know what might end up becoming your passion. Here are some suggestions for you to try . . .

Gymnastics

Zumba

Skateboarding

Yoga

Dance

Badminton

Hiking/walking

Tennis

Football

Pilates

Table tennis

Biking

Skating

Build exercise into your day-to-day life

There are loads of fun and free ways you can incorporate more exercise into your life. Here are some suggestions . . .

- Walk or scooter to school and back
- Have fun with your friends by making up dance routines
- Go for runs with your parent or carer
- Suggest going out for a walk as a family – lots of adults aren't getting enough exercise either so this could help you all become healthier
- Help with the gardening
- Play games of chase with younger siblings
- Go cycling as a family

How much exercise should you get?

The government recommends that young people between the ages of five and eighteen should engage in moderate-to-vigorous intensity physical activity for an average of 60 minutes per day across the week. You'll notice these three changes in your body when doing moderate activity . . .

- Your body will become warmer
- Your heart will beat faster
- You'll become a little bit out of breath but still able to have a conversation

Examples of moderate activity are walking and cycling. If you're so out of breath that you aren't able to have a conversation, it means you're taking vigorous exercise. Vigorous activity includes playing a sport, dancing and swimming.

Diet and nutrition

Another thing that's so important when it comes to our health is our diet. The food we eat is our fuel, but while it's important to pay attention to the type of food we eat, it's also important that we grow up with a healthy relationship with food. Eating is about sitting down and socialising with friends and family. Food is also a cultural thing. Imagine birthdays or Christmas or other religious celebrations without food – pretty grim, right? I cannot imagine a life without cake in it, so here's to eating for health and for fun – in moderation of course!

What is a healthy diet?

First things first, a healthy diet is made up of different food groups known as carbohydrates, protein, fruit and vegetables, dairy or dairy substitutes and fat.

One third of the food you eat every day should be fruit and veg, and another third should be carbohydrates. The final third should be made up of dairy or dairy alternatives, protein and healthy fat.

The Eatwell Guide has a handy example of what a balanced diet looks like. It was put together by nutrition experts and scientists to advise us on the kinds of foods we should be eating day to day – there are plenty of yummy things in there; take a look at this helpful visual guide below:

FRUIT AND VEG

CARBOHYDRATES

FAT

PROTEIN SOURCES

DAIRY AND
DAIRY ALTERNATIVES

Here are a few simple tips when considering each food group . . .

Carbohydrates

Carbohydrates include breakfast cereals, rice, pasta, baked goods and potatoes, and they are really good sources of energy. Where possible try to eat the wholegrain option. Wholegrains contain all the nutrition, keep you fuller longer, help digestion and can even prevent heart disease and some cancers.

Brown rice, wholemeal flour and cereals like Weetabix and Shredded Wheat are perfect examples of wholegrain carbs with no added sugar.

Fruit and veg

We should consume at least five portions of fruit and veg a day. One portion is roughly a fist size. I know this can be difficult as you probably don't have a huge amount of choice over what you eat. But I bet if you ask your parents to buy more fruit and veg, they'll probably be overjoyed!

I also recommend that you ask to have a fruit bowl visible in your kitchen. If you can see the fruit, you're far more likely to reach for it when you're looking for a snack.

Why not offer to take on the role of making a salad bowl to go with dinner? That way you're benefiting the whole family. Embrace your role as Queen of the Salad Bowl – get creative by adding nuts and fruit and experimenting with salad dressing.

Protein sources

This food group is really important in helping you grow and repair your muscles and stay strong. Meat is high in protein but we live in a world where many people are trying to consume less of it and are becoming vegetarian or vegan. The great news is there are many other ways to get protein, such as beans, eggs, legumes such as chickpeas, and tofu.

Dairy and dairy alternatives

These are great sources of calcium, which is really important for keeping your bones nice and strong. Your bones grow stronger throughout your childhood, but by the end of your teens most of the opportunity to create bone strength is lost. It's so important to know this now, so you can reduce your risk of osteoporosis later on.

Osteoporosis is a health condition that causes bones to become weak and at risk of breaking easily.

The reason I want to talk about this condition in this book is because it affects so many women – more than one in three will sustain one or more osteoporotic bone fractures in their lifetime.

Women are at greater risk of osteoporosis due to the loss of bone density caused by menopause. Menopause is when oestrogen hormone levels rapidly drop and periods stop. It's normal and usually happens to women in their late forties or early fifties. While we're talking about it, you should also know the word 'perimenopause', which is the months or years leading up to menopause when women may start to have menopausal symptoms.

You might be wondering why I'm telling you this now. It's because you can take action in your teenage years to help prevent osteoporosis by making sure you have a calcium-rich diet.

The best source of calcium comes from cow's milk and dairy products. So if you are able to drink cow's milk, this would be the preference over plant-based milks. Aim to have some dairy in your diet every day.

If you are vegan or can't eat dairy products, you can get calcium from other foods such as seeds, sardines, almonds, beans and lentils. If you do drink plant-based milk, make sure it is fortified with calcium and not sweetened with added sugar.

Another way to optimise the density of your bones is exercise, and more specifically exercise that puts some form of shock or jolting through your bones. When we jump up and down, for example, it signals to our bones to get stronger. So simply jumping up and down on the spot twenty times a day would do the job. Running, dancing and energetic sports will do the trick too.

Fat

When it comes to diet, fat gets a bad press, but we need fat for energy and it also keeps our hearts and brains healthy – as long as it's the right type of fat. Healthy or 'good' fats include olive oil, avocado, nuts, oily fish (e.g. salmon, mackerel, sardines), and sunflower and pumpkin seeds. Less healthy fats are found in fried and processed foods like fish and chips and pizza, and in shop-bought cakes and pastries, red meat, butter and ice cream.

Water

It's easy to forget about water but it's so important to stay hydrated. You should aim to drink between six and eight glasses of water a day.

Unhealthy diets and eating disorders

Restricting what we eat because of how we want to look or allowing things to get in the way of our enjoyment of food can lead to lifelong issues with eating and weight. It's important to know that what we eat, how we feel and our body image are linked, and it can be a bit of a battle for some people. Which is why it's important to make sure we try to focus on keeping healthy, ensuring that the food we fuel ourselves with is balanced, and not to fixate on how we look on the outside. This is the core part of having a healthy relationship with food. However, if you feel pressured to control your diet or starve yourself in the hope that you might look a certain way, there is help out there.

Eating disorders, such as anorexia, bulimia and binge eating, are when someone uses the control of food as a way of coping with their feelings and other situations.

If you're really struggling with your eating, I would encourage you to contact your GP with the help of an adult or caregiver.

Food insecurity

I grew up in a house where we didn't have much money for food, but I'm grateful that my mum was a good cook and able to work miracles with very little. At the start of the week she'd go to the freezer shop and buy a big bag of frozen mince and a big bag of frozen peppers, and she'd somehow make that stretch for three or four days, making shepherd's pie, spaghetti bolognese, lasagne and chilli.

One in four households in the UK with children experienced food insecurity in September 2022 – affecting 4 million children. It is awful that so many families are living in poverty, but there is absolutely nothing shameful about needing to rely on food banks or qualifying for free school meals. And if you do qualify for free school meals, this is a great opportunity to bulk up on fruit and veg by choosing the healthy option.

The food writer and journalist Jack Monroe has also done loads of great work when it comes to helping people eat healthily on a really tight budget, making sure people are able to get all the nutrients they need. You can find some great recipes on her website, where she breaks down exactly how much – or how little – each recipe cost to make, including her infamous banana bread, which is super cheap and delicious.

What you put in your body

It's not just the food you put in your body that affects your physical health – substances such as alcohol, and smoking and vaping all have an impact too.

Smoking

Thankfully there has been a steady decline in the number of people who smoke and most young people are much too clever to even try it. Which is lucky, as smoking is more harmful to young people than to adults because their lungs and airways aren't fully developed yet, and smoking while young can reduce your lung growth and your maximum lung function in the future.

It is also highly addictive and can cause serious harm to your long-term health. Not only can smoking cause cancer and other serious illnesses such as heart disease, but nicotine, the addictive ingredient in cigarettes, has been linked to anxiety too.

If a friend is pressuring you to smoke you just need to say . . . *'Thanks for offering but that's just not my vibe.'*

Vaping

So what about vaping instead? Even though vaping is less harmful
than smoking tobacco there have been cases of people becoming
seriously ill from it. Vaping can cause lung damage by exposing your
lungs to chemicals, and if you vape with nicotine, you could
become addicted. So if you're being pressured to vape,
take the same advice I offered about smoking and say:
'Thanks for offering but that's just not my vibe.'

Alcohol

Drinking alcohol before the age of eighteen can also have serious
consequences for your health as it can affect the development
of your vital organs and functions, including your bones, liver
and brain. It also puts you more at risk of dangerous behaviour,
such as drug-taking or violence.

I know it can be really hard to say no if you're being pressured
by friends to drink, smoke or vape, but you only get one
wonderful body – it makes so much sense to take care of
it while you're still growing and developing. Your future,
older self will thank you for it later, trust me!

Dental health

OK, so now we're feeling fit and healthy and have looked at what to put – and what not to put – into our body. But what about the other aspects of our health? They might not be something we think about all the time but our teeth are incredibly important when it comes to our health. It's not just how they look – by keeping our teeth clean, we can also avoid bad breath and other diseases.

Thankfully, we've come a long way when it comes to our dental health care. Did you know that before the invention of fillings, people would have their teeth pulled out if they got a cavity? So there were a lot of toothless people walking about! And before the invention of toothpaste, people would use things like ground oyster shells and pulverised bricks to clean their teeth. And in Germany in the Middle Ages it was believed that toothache could only be cured by kissing a donkey!

CURED WITH
A KISS

Thankfully you won't need to kiss any donkeys nowadays to keep your teeth healthy. Simply follow my tips below . . .

- Brush your teeth for at least two minutes twice a day, in the morning and just before bed, and floss daily from the age of twelve

- Use a fluoride toothpaste to help keep your teeth and enamel strong

- Visit your dentist regularly

- Avoid exposing your teeth to sugars and acid outside of mealtimes – if you're grazing between meals, food can get stuck in your teeth and cause decay

- Lemon or lime in water with a meal is OK but between meals it can damage the enamel on your teeth – think about putting a sprig of mint or rosemary or a slice of cucumber in your water instead

Sleep

So we've eaten dinner, brushed our teeth and now it's bedtime. Phew. I'm exhausted. A good night's sleep really is the best prescription for keeping well that I can give you. Why? Well . . .

- It gives you the energy to live your life to the fullest

- It improves your concentration and performance at school and in sports

- It helps your mental health – sleep deprivation has been linked to depression

- It boosts your immune system

- It improves your relationships because you're in better control of your emotions

- It's linked to healthy weight

- Over a lifetime it reduces the risk of diabetes and heart disease

See, sleep is pretty awesome – keeping us recharged, healthy and energised. So, exactly how much sleep do you need?

Between the ages of eight and twelve, you need 10 to 11 hours of sleep a night. But as you get older, hormone changes can affect your sleep patterns. Once puberty kicks in, you will probably start getting tired later – at 10 or 11 p.m. rather than 8 or 9 p.m.

The trouble is, you're still expected to get up at the same time for school, so it's natural that you'll feel tired and want to lie in. Your parents may think you're being lazy or staying up late on purpose but it's actually scientifically proven that your body naturally wants to go to bed later and lie in in the morning. As you're not able to have a lie-in on school days, it's really important that you catch up on sleep at the weekend. Tell your parents you have my permission (doctor's orders).

The good news is that some schools are experimenting with making the school day start and end later for teens so that they can be in class when their brain has woken up and is ready to learn. But until all schools make these changes, here are my tips for getting as much sleep as possible . . .

Avoid screens

I know it might seem bizarre that looking at a screen stops us from falling asleep but the trouble is, our brains can't tell the difference between the blue light from a screen and daylight. When it starts getting dark, our brain releases a hormone called melatonin, which makes us feel all nice and sleepy. But if we're exposed to blue light at night our brain thinks it's still daytime and this is prevented. It's also good to give your eyes a break. So, to get your brain and body ready for sleep, turn your devices off at least half an hour before going to bed.

Sleep routine

Unfortunately you can't just get into bed and order your body to go to sleep, but you can train it to know when it's time to fall asleep by having a sleep routine. To help you wind down, I recommend you start this routine 30 to 60 minutes before sleep, doing one or more of the following . . .

- Read a book for 20 minutes
- Have a bath
- Have a camomile tea or milky drink
- Meditate (you can find more info on how to do this in chapter 7)

It's a bit like training a dog to know its walkies time whenever you fetch its lead. If you follow the same routine every night, your body will recognise that it's time to go to sleep.

Make your bedroom sleep ready

Chances are you use your bedroom for many things – like doing your homework, scrolling online, hanging out with friends and plotting the downfall of an annoying sibling! But it's also really important that your brain associates your bedroom with going to sleep. Before going to bed, aim for a room temperature of around 17 to 18 degrees Celsius if you can, shut the blinds or curtains and put any devices and homework away.

CHAPTER 5

FAMILY AND FRIENDSHIPS

LET ME ASK YOU A QUESTION . . .

What's the most important relationship you have? Most people would probably say it's with their mum, dad, sibling or best friend. But actually the most important relationship of your life is the one you have with yourself. I didn't realise this when I was younger, and throughout my teenage years I was very self-critical and lacked self-belief. I constantly searched for my faults and doubted everything about myself from my appearance to my sporting and academic ability. I really wish I knew then what I know now and had focused on being more loving to myself.

That said, we are social creatures after all and our relationships with other people are really important and can take a lot of work. In this chapter I'm going to show you how to have the healthiest, best possible relationships with the people in your life, from your parents to your friends, and even your crushes!

Parents

No two families are identical and we all have different relationships with our parents. Some parents are still together, some are divorced and others are separated, and many people today are living in blended families, with step-parents and step-siblings. As young kids we tend to think that our parents are perfect and right about everything, but once we start growing up, they can fall from that pedestal. As you've grown older your friends have probably started becoming more important to you, and you feel you have more in common with them than with your parents. It's totally normal for you to start wanting more independence during puberty. It's also totally normal to suddenly start finding certain people annoying. Don't forget, you're currently riding a hormonal rollercoaster and that can definitely affect the way you react to people.

You may feel like some of your friends have cooler parents than yours – and chances are, some of them will have parents who are stricter than yours too! It's all fine; no type of parent is better than the other. You might not be able to change your parents but remember, they do have your best interests at heart and they are on your side. They also might be a little hurt that you no longer have them on a pedestal and have started to find them annoying. I know it's hard but try to remember that parents are people too. If you've not been seeing eye to eye with your parents and you want to improve your relationship, try the following exercise.

Three reasons

Write down three reasons why you should be allowed to do whatever it is you've been arguing about, for example having a sleepover at a friend's on a school night. Then put yourself in your parents' point of view and write down three reasons why they might not want you to. Then, when you're feeling calm, tell them why you understand their reasoning, but put forward the reasons you think you should be allowed to go. This will show them you're considering both sides of the argument and trying to find a resolution. They still might not agree but will appreciate you being mature about it and might be more relaxed next time you ask.

Divorce

There might be times when parents have to separate or split up because they can no longer live with each other. Sadly, sometimes things just don't work out, and it may not be anyone's fault.

Some divorces are handled well but for many families it can be a really challenging time. My parents divorced when I was five and it was really hard. While I always knew that they both loved me, they didn't go about things in a mature way. There were lots of arguments and a court battle over custody and the house. My parents had a lot of bad feeling towards each other, which wasn't nice for me as a child. But when I look back, I can see that my parents were still really young when they got divorced, and I'm sure if they had the wisdom that I have now they wouldn't have behaved in that way.

If your parents are going through a break-up or divorce, here are some tips to help you feel better . . .

- The most important thing to remember is that it isn't your fault and things will improve with time – it can just take a little while to get used to and for things to settle

- If your parents' arguments are upsetting you, let them know and ask them if they can discuss things when you're not around

- Speaking to another trusted adult such as a teacher or school counsellor, or an older sibling about what's happening can really help

- Another great way to get things off your chest is to write about how you're feeling in a journal

Addiction

Another issue that can affect your relationship with your family is if they are suffering from an addiction. If your parent has a drink or drug problem, it can feel as if they love the thing they're addicted to more than they love you, which can be really painful. The important thing to remember is that addiction is an illness, so you mustn't take it personally.

My mum developed what could be described as 'problem drinking' when I was fourteen. Prior to that she just drank socially, although she always found it difficult to know when to stop.

I moved out of home when I was seventeen because it was so difficult living with her drinking. I often used to feel as if she loved drinking more than she loved me. Once I even picked up her bottle of vodka and asked her which she would choose, alcohol or me. Now I know that addiction is an illness so this wasn't a fair question to ask her, but as a young person I didn't understand.

If your parent has a problem with drinking, here's some advice . . .

- Firstly, if you ever feel unsafe due to your parent's drinking, because it makes them violent or aggressive, it's really important to seek help from a trusted adult – or contact Childline and ask their advice

- Remember that your parent's drinking isn't your fault or responsibility

- If their drinking upsets you, try to avoid being around it

- Talk to another trusted adult or older sibling about how you're feeling – your feelings matter and it's so important that you're able to express them

Tips for living in a stressful family

It might not just be a parent's drinking or addiction that can cause stress; there are many things that can really take a toll on a family. We can't control our parents', carers' or siblings' behaviour but we can control how much we let it get to us. Hopefully these tips can help you deal with a stressful home life . . .

- Take exercise, like going for a walk or a run. It gets you out of the house and gives you a break, with the added bonus of releasing feel-good chemicals in your brain. Just make sure you tell your parents where you're going, and if it's dark, stay in your garden or try an indoor workout to get your blood pumping

- Keep reminding yourself that it's not personal and it's not your fault. Your parents don't hate you and even if you didn't exist, their issues would still be happening

- See or call a friend and talk about it with them. Sharing a problem can often help you feel a bit better about it. They might be experiencing something similar too

- Put your earbuds in and listen to calming music or a relaxation meditation (you can find loads for free on YouTube)

- Talk to your parents about how you're feeling when they're calm. It might be that they genuinely don't know the effect their behaviour is having on you. If it's easier, write this in a letter to them

- Journaling your feelings on paper can really help, especially if your thoughts are whirling round in your brain at night, preventing you from falling asleep

Friendships

Have you heard the saying 'friends are the family you get to choose'? I love this saying because it sums up how important our friendships are. You might have already noticed certain changes in your friendships as you enter puberty. Some friends may have become closer and others might have drifted away. It's all OK. As you grow up your interests can change and you find you have less in common with certain friends.

Let's take a look at what makes a good friend and what to do when a friendship ends . . .

How to be a good friend

If you really care about someone then being a good friend will probably come automatically, but just in case you need a reminder, here are my ingredients for being a great friend . . .

- You're able to put yourself in their shoes and understand them
- You're a good listener
- You're there for them when they need you
- You don't avoid them if they're going through something that feels a bit uncomfortable
- You can be trusted with their secrets
- You have their best interests at heart

- You enjoy making them feel happy
- You like doing things with them
- You appreciate your differences as well as your similarities

Finding your tribe

Finding your tribe means finding other people who are like you in some way. It's so important to be true to yourself and not try to fit in with a certain group of people just because you think you should. Remember, you might not find your tribe right away, so don't panic – it can take a bit of time. Sometimes friendships can even come out of the most unexpected places; you just need to be open-minded.

Peer pressure can feel like a *lot*, but if you're feeling pressured into doing things you don't want to with people you don't want to hang out with, there are things you can do to get out of it . . .

- Practise saying no firmly
- Tell them your parents won't let you
- Make up an excuse that you have to be somewhere else

When like-minded people come together, amazing things can happen and you can make friends for life. You might share an interest, like saving the environment, or a passion for a sport, art or other activity. Whatever it is, you're much more likely to succeed and have a good time if you're doing it with people who have the same goal as you.

The first tribe I belonged to was my rugby team and if I had to sum up in just one word how this tribe made me feel it would be 'safe'. Rugby brought us all together and because we were all different shapes and sizes, sexualities, ethnicities and from different social backgrounds, it broke down so many barriers. A couple of the girls were closer to the Queen than they were to me in terms of social status and I remember one of them telling me that I was her first ever black friend. But when we came together none of it mattered.

We were a team and we were all equally important and we all looked out for each other like a family.

Finding your tribe is like finding a family that you have chosen; a family that loves and accepts you just as you are, making you feel safe and supported.

Dr Zoe's Prescription

Take the first step

If you haven't found your tribe yet, please don't worry. It took me a while. Make a list of your interests and passions – such as sports, music, arts, books, political issues, other activities. Then ask your parent or caregiver to help you do a search to see if you can find any groups you could join – either online or in your area. Or join an after-school club. Don't be afraid to try something random. I know it can be nerve-wracking taking that first step but being brave can really pay off, as finding your tribe can change everything for the better.

Friendship red flags

One minute you think you've met your soul sister, a true Best Friend Forever, but then you start getting a weird, uneasy feeling and what was a fun friendship becomes stressful. Sometimes friendships are not what they seem and some friends are fair-weather, not forever. But don't worry, I'm here to help you spot some of the red flags. If you find yourself with a friend like this it might be time to move on . . .

- They drop you when someone else comes along
- They make you feel bad and put you down
- They talk about you behind your back
- They always put their feelings first
- They put pressure on you and don't listen to you
- They're only there for you when things are going well

When a friendship ends

When I asked my question at the start of this chapter, I'm sure many of you will have thought that your most important relationships are with your friends. When things are going well, it can feel as if our friends are closer than our family. But sometimes friendships can change and even end, and that can be devastating. When a friendship ends, you can feel a real mixture of emotions, from anger to sadness and from jealousy to disappointment, which can all come at once and feel overwhelming.

Often, the end of a friendship can be our very first big break-up, so it can be hard to believe that you'll ever get over the feeling of heartbreak and rejection.

If you've experienced a friendship break-up, you have to remember that you can't control other people's actions but you *can* control your own reactions.

Focus on nurturing your relationship with yourself and always be kind and graceful. Don't try to get your own back — you'll only hurt yourself more.

There can also be the tendency to blame yourself, but it really isn't a reflection of you as a person. Unless of course you did do something to hurt the other person. If that's the case, then owning up to your part in it and apologising can make a huge positive difference. I know the thought of doing that might make you cringe, but trust me, you'll feel so much better about yourself and the situation if you find the courage to say sorry.

Sometimes friendships can end over a misunderstanding. If you think this has happened to you, it's well worth trying to talk about it to clear the air and see if you can salvage the friendship.

The first major friendship break-up I had really made me doubt myself and think that it must have been my fault, that there was something wrong with me. I really let it get to me and knock my confidence.

It's OK to be upset and cry and show your feelings. Crying doesn't mean you're depressed, and you're allowed to feel sad. But if your sadness starts to feel overwhelming, try doing the following . . .

- Keep busy
- Do things that make you feel good
- Spend time with people who love you
- Re-read the chapter in this book on confidence
- Talk to a parent, carer or older sibling about how you're feeling

Being bullied

Bullying. That horrible word. Bullying is the worst. It can take many forms – it can be physical or name-calling or even online – and when it happens, it can feel like the most terrible thing in the world.

SIGNS THAT YOU ARE BEING BULLIED
- They hurt you physically or threaten to hurt you
- They call you names and repeatedly make fun of you
- They say negative things about you to other people or online
- They exclude you from a group of people
- They insult you based on your appearance, gender, ethnicity or disability
- You feel physically sick at the thought of having to see them

If you're being bullied, it's so important that you speak to an adult and ask for help. Tell a parent or teacher so something can be done about it. And remember to be kind and compassionate to yourself. The bullies want to try and pull you down and damage your self-confidence, so you need to do all you can to counteract that.

Being subjected to bullying is awful and understanding why someone is a bully isn't going to fix things, but there's usually a reason, like they themselves lack confidence, are feeling jealous of you or are having a difficult time at home. Their need to put others down is definitely a symptom that something's not right in their life and it's a cry for help. Talk to someone about how you're feeling, but try to remember that this is not your fault and the problem is with them, not you.

IF YOU ARE THE BULLY

If you've been bullying other people, you may already be starting to see why what you're doing is wrong. The important thing to realise is that you don't have to keep on being a bully; you can change. If you need support and help to do this, don't be afraid to ask a trusted adult for it. It's not always easy to do, or to do immediately. The only way to heal the wounds of the person you've bullied is by saying sorry to them, and trust me, it will help you heal too.

Prejudice

Some forms of bullying are rooted in prejudice. We're all different and the things that make us different can be our strengths but can also pose some challenges.

It can be all too easy to become prejudiced against another person or group of people because they're different to you. People can be prejudiced against others because of things like their weight, age, religion, class, race and skin colour.

I was the only mixed-race girl in a predominantly white school, so I was always very aware of being different. When I was forming relationships, the fear that I might be judged for my difference was always at the back of my mind. My mum was white and she tried to protect my brother and me by telling us that any people who were mean to us were just jealous. When I look back now, I can see that she was preparing us for the racism we were bound to experience at some point.

Prejudice isn't always down to jealousy; it can be caused by ignorance and fear of the unknown too. Sometimes it's as obvious as calling someone a racist name, but other times it can be more subtle. These are called microaggressions, and they can take the form of jokes, casual remarks or loaded questions. They might not be as obvious but they can be just as hurtful.

We all have a responsibility to take action to eliminate racism and other forms of prejudice. It's about being brave enough to decide that you won't tolerate it. And this isn't just at school – it could be at home with your parents, siblings, cousins or other family members.

If someone says something that makes you feel uncomfortable, let them know. You don't have to get into an argument with them, you could just say something like: 'I didn't like it when you said that. It made me feel sad/uncomfortable.'

We all have the right to say out loud how something makes us feel. If you don't feel confident enough to speak out, at the very least you should ignore what they say and don't react or go along with it. Our differences shouldn't make us feel afraid or suspicious. If you can learn to embrace them, they could make for some really interesting and rich friendships. I have friends who are Hindu and celebrate Diwali. My nephew's mum is Muslim and celebrates Eid. The more different cultures you surround yourself with, the more chances you'll have to join in with their fun celebrations, *and* you'll have way more opportunities to eat cake – always a very good thing in my opinion!

Embrace diversity and let it enrich your life.

Dr Zoe's Prescription

Be curious

Is there someone in your school who's from a different background to you? Make the effort to get to know them better by asking them some genuine, heartfelt questions. They'll probably be really flattered that you asked and you could end up making a really interesting friend.

CHAPTER 6

SEX, SEXUALITY AND RELATIONSHIPS

DUN DUN DUUUUN, YEP, WE'RE HERE, AT THE *WHISPERS* SEX CHAPTER . . .

The main thing I remember about sex education in schools is that it was really embarrassing. Even the teacher seemed embarrassed, which made it even worse. All I could think was, *Please let this be over!* The topic of sex can feel very awkward, especially when grown-ups talk about it. However, it is something that you're likely to become increasingly interested in as you grow older and it becomes very important to people in their teens. The trouble is, if

you aren't able to talk freely with your parents or teachers about sex it can leave you open to less reliable sources of information.

So let's talk about sex openly here, and if it doesn't feel relevant to you right now you can always keep this book and come back to this chapter when you do want more information.

Let's start with the basics: **What is sex? And what is the difference between sex and gender?**

Confusingly, sex has two meanings. The first and most common use for the word sex is when you are describing whether someone is a girl or a boy.

The word gender has a similar meaning, but while sex refers to the body parts you were born with, gender is more to do with a person's identity, in other words whether they feel like a boy or a girl. For most people their sex and gender identity will always be the same, but for a small number of people, as they grow up they realise that their gender identity is different from their biological sex (or 'sex assigned at birth').

So for example, their birth certificate might say girl, but as they get older, they realise that they identify as a boy, or vice versa. This may mean they are transgender.

The other meaning of Sex

The other definition of sex means taking part in sexual activity and sexual intercourse.

In general terms sex is when two people of any gender involve themselves in activities where there is penetration of the vagina (vaginal sex), the anus (anal sex) or the mouth (oral sex). First things first, it is illegal for people under the age of sixteen in the UK to have sex, and this is to protect you from doing something you don't want to do or might regret later.

The biological reason for men and women to have sex is to reproduce. But that's not the only reason people have sex or even the most common. People have sex for pleasure too, as a way of feeling intimate with another person, for fun and to feel good. It's a natural activity that lots of grown-ups do.

But sometimes people have sex for the wrong reasons – they might be trying to get someone to like them, or they might feel like they should have sex even though they don't really want to, or they're being pressured to do so. And sometimes sex can happen without a person's consent.

So let's dig a little deeper and make sure we understand what sex is, when it is healthy, why it isn't at all embarrassing and what precautions need to be taken once you're old enough to start thinking about doing it.

Self-pleasure

Before you even start considering having sex, it's normal and healthy to begin to explore your own body first. As you grow up you might start to notice that it feels good to touch your body in certain places and that's absolutely fine.

Masturbation is touching or rubbing the genitals for sexual pleasure and it's a totally normal part of sexual development. Girls masturbate by touching and rubbing their clitoris, vulva and vagina (the inner canal), and boys masturbate by touching and rubbing their penis. It can feel nice to do this, and exploring your body is part of growing up, though some people hardly ever masturbate, and some don't do it at all. It's all normal.

Our bodies are so wonderful and clever, and every bit of our anatomy is there for a reason. Your body is yours. You own it and you have more right to look at it and touch it and explore it than anyone else.

The clitoris

The clitoris is the most sensitive part of the female genitals and the primary source of sexual pleasure for women and girls. Because female self-pleasure hasn't been spoken about much, most people aren't familiar with the anatomy of the clitoris.

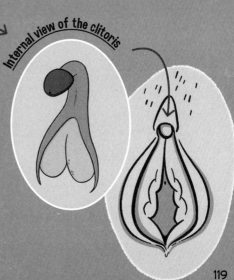

Internal view of the clitoris

MYTH BUSTER

People don't tend to talk about masturbation much and this has led to certain untruths being said about it, including that . . .

- Only boys masturbate
- Masturbation will stop you from having children
- Masturbation could give you an STI
- Masturbation will affect your periods
- Masturbation causes blindness, cancer or mental illness

I can tell you as a doctor that none of these myths are true and in fact masturbation is good for you! The benefits can include . . .

- Relieving stress
- Helping sleep
- Improving self-esteem and body image

Babies

So we now know that sex isn't just about making babies
– people do it for fun and pleasure when they are in
healthy grown-up relationships. But biologically, sex
is the reason we all exist. Babies are made when
a man and woman have penetrative vaginal sex
and a sperm from the man meets an egg from the
woman. Here's what happens in a little more detail . . .

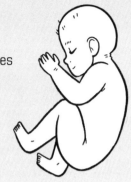

When the man is sexually aroused, his penis fills with blood, which
makes it go hard. This is called an erection. Changes happen to the
woman's body as well. As she gets aroused her labia and genitals
become more sensitive and swollen and she will release a natural
lubricant.

The man inserts his penis into the vagina and when he has an
orgasm, fluid containing sperm (the male reproductive cell, which is
made in the testicles) travels from his testicles through his penis
into the vagina. This is called ejaculation. Although women orgasm
too, they don't ejaculate in this way.

The fluid travels through the woman's vagina and into her womb and
fallopian tubes. In order for a baby to be made, the sperm must
meet an egg which has been released from the woman's ovary. Only

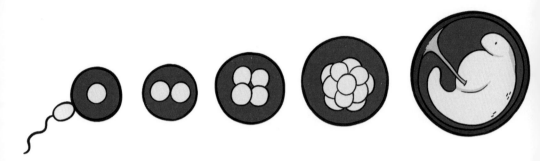

then can fertilisation occur and a potential embryo develop, which will grow over time into a baby.

It takes nine months for a baby to become fully grown in the womb. This is known as pregnancy. After around 40 weeks the woman will give birth to her baby.

Fertility and other ways of having babies/children

Girls are born with all the eggs we'll ever have already inside of us. Amazing, right?! And as we go through life that number of eggs starts to fall. The likelihood of pregnancy starts to slowly drop at the age of twenty-five and after thirty-five it rapidly reduces. Some women will even experience early menopause (where oestrogen hormone levels rapidly drop and their periods stop). This usually happens when a woman is in their late forties or earlier fifties, but one in a hundred stop their periods before the age of forty and one in a thousand before the age of thirty.

Of course, this isn't the only way people can have babies. Gay couples or couples who are struggling to conceive can try IVF, fostering, adoption and surrogacy. Some people also choose to have a baby without a partner – this is called solo parenting.

IVF – stands for in vitro fertilisation and is when an egg is fertilised by sperm outside of the body and then implanted into the uterus

Fostering – foster carers provide a safe home for children who aren't able to stay with their own family

Adoption – when someone becomes the legal parent of a child that isn't biologically theirs

Surrogacy – when a woman agrees to have a baby for a couple who will become the baby's parents after it's born

Safety first

Contraception

One thing you will be guaranteed to learn about in sex education is the risk of pregnancy if you have unprotected vaginal sex. When I was at school, teen pregnancy was fairly common and a number of girls in my year left early to have babies. The rates of teen pregnancy have fallen since then and this is largely due to increased access to contraception.

There are many different types of contraception, including . . .

- **Contraceptive pill** – a daily pill that stops ovulation

- **IUD** – a small T-shaped device inserted into the uterus

- **Implant** – a small plastic rod inserted under the skin of the upper arm

- **Diaphragm** – a shallow silicone cup inserted into the vagina before sex

- **Injections** – an injection that releases progesterone into the bloodstream

- **Condoms** – a thin rubber sheath worn on the penis during sex, which stops a man's ejaculate from getting inside his partner

These all have differing levels of effectiveness at preventing pregnancy, but the most effective at preventing both pregnancy and the spread of sexually transmitted infections (STIs) is a condom. Condoms can be bought from supermarkets and chemists, unlike other forms of contraception which need to be issued by your healthcare professional.

Sexually transmitted infections

Another thing you have to consider when thinking about having a sexual relationship with someone is STIs. There are a number of different infections that can be transmitted through sex, including . . .

- Chlamydia
- Gonorrhoea
- Genital warts
- Genital herpes
- Pubic lice
- HIV

Chlamydia is the most common STI among young people and can cause damage to the fallopian tubes in women, which can make it more difficult or even impossible to get pregnant when you do eventually want to have a baby.

At least 70 per cent of women who get chlamydia don't experience any symptoms. But for those who do, symptoms include . . .

- Unusual vaginal discharge
- Pain during sex
- Pain while urinating
- Pain in the pelvis or tummy
- Bleeding after sex
- Bleeding between periods

Chlamydia is easily treated with antibiotics. If you're worried about STIs, make an appointment at your doctor's surgery or sexual health clinic to be tested, and any partners should get tested too. There's nothing to be ashamed about and it's definitely better to be on the safe side.

Consent

Consent is needed for every type of sexual activity, including kissing and touching parts of another person's body, as well as sex itself. And consent is needed *every* time, so if you've kissed someone before, you still have the right to say no to them in the future.

When I was young, I went on a date with an older boy to the cinema. He'd snuck some alcohol in and I got quite drunk. Halfway through the film I went to the toilet and he followed me in and tried to kiss me. I pushed him off but he kept laughing and making a joke out of it as if I was only play-fighting. In the end I had to yell, 'No, get off me!' to let him know that I really meant it. This was someone I knew and trusted, so I was really upset when it happened and a bit embarrassed too. When things like this happen, some people don't always want to make a big deal out of it and almost find it easier to go along with something they don't want to because they don't want to make a fuss. But as far as I'm concerned, unless you are feeling **a hundred per cent 'yes, yes, yes'** about doing something, then it has to be **'no, no, no!'**

If the other person still doesn't get the message, tell them that no means no. Try to move away from them or ask someone nearby for help. Your body belongs to you and you only, and no one has the right to be intimate with you unless they have your permission. If they don't, this is deemed as sexual abuse.

Sexual abuse

Sexual abuse is when someone is forced, pressurised or tricked into taking part in any form of sexual activity. This might be by someone they know and could even be a family member. If reading this chapter makes you realise that you are being or have been sexually abused, or you know someone that has, it's so important that you tell someone. What's happened is in no way your fault, you're not alone and there are lots of people who can help you. Talk to a trusted adult, and if you feel awkward or embarrassed about telling them what's happened you could always write it down in a letter to them. If you don't feel comfortable telling an adult you know, you can always contact Childline (see the resources section at the back of this book), either online or over the phone.

Online porn

Online porn is so prevalent that even if you don't feel ready you may already be aware of it. It's so important you understand that online porn is not real sex and nothing like real life. The women in porn videos often wear ridiculous underwear and loads of make-up and heels, and most porn videos only show one type of vulva with very small labia. The penises featured also tend to be way larger than typical. The type of sex and positions also tend to be nothing like real life. Basically everything about online porn is fake, so if you do ever see any please bear this in mind.

If you have seen something sexual online that has caused you concern, please speak to a trusted adult or parent about it. When it comes to sex, the most important thing to remember is that it's your body and anything you do with it should be on your terms, when you feel ready – and not a moment before. It's also important to realise that some people will lie about being sexually experienced because they want to seem more grown-up and knowledgeable, but it's not a race. You are totally entitled to live your life at your own pace.

Crushes

One minute they're just another classmate in school – then suddenly you can't stop thinking about them and wanting to see them at *every possible opportunity*. And when you do see them, your heart races and butterflies start fluttering in your tummy. Welcome to your first crush!

It's totally normal to have crushes when you're growing up. I had a mega crush on an actor who was in a TV show every Sunday. I used to sit there watching it with my family, blushing away. I even used to imagine he was sending messages to me through the camera! Trust me, your brain can do crazy things if you really like someone and want them to like you too. And you can feel heartbroken if they don't look in your direction.

During puberty, you can develop crushes on people of the opposite sex or of the same sex – or both. This doesn't necessarily mean that you're gay (attracted to members of the same sex) or straight (attracted to members of the opposite sex). As you get older, you'll see a pattern develop when it comes to who you're attracted to. It's easy for older people to trivialise crushes, but when you are experiencing them, they feel really important and overwhelming. And if you have a crush on someone in your school it can be a major distraction and even affect your academic performance.

If you're struggling with how your crush is making you feel, try journaling about it or talking to a friend you can trust. Chances are they'll be experiencing a crush of their own too. One of the hardest things about crushes is the realisation that they probably won't go anywhere — especially if your crush is on a celebrity or older boy at school. But please don't worry, you're not alone! And please don't worry if you haven't experienced a crush yet — like everything else in puberty, it's totally normal to experience different things at different times.

Shhhh, overshare moment . . .

My brother is three years older than me and when I was young I had crushes on several of his friends. This was highly embarrassing for him, especially because I would send them love letters (years before you could slide into anyone's DMs). While my crushes were very real and very intense at the time, I can confidently say that by the time I was sixteen I had absolutely no interest in any of them. In fact . . . Ewww!

Sexuality and attraction

A person's sexuality or sexual orientation is defined according to the gender or genders they are attracted to. Sometimes girls fancy boys, sometimes girls fancy girls and sometimes they fancy both.

- Attracted to opposite sex = straight, heterosexual
- Attracted to same sex = lesbian, homosexual, gay
- Attracted to both sexes = bisexual

If you find that you're attracted to someone unexpectedly, be curious about it – don't be embarrassed or ashamed. When you're young, it can be hard to know whether you're attracted to someone or you simply admire them and want to be like them. This is all fine. As you get older, you'll start to see a pattern forming and you'll be able to figure out your sexual identity.

Attraction plays a key role in making people come together and stay together in relationships, but chances are you'll start feeling attracted to people long before you feel ready for a relationship. Signs that you're attracted to someone include getting a funny feeling in your tummy, feeling like you want to kiss them and getting nervous around them.

You might be attracted to someone for the way they look, the way they act, who they are or what they do, like being a popstar.

Developing feelings of attraction towards someone for the first time can be very intense, but try not to feel overwhelmed. These feelings will fade with time and you'll probably move on to be attracted to someone else. It's all part of your body and brain growing up and getting ready for the day when you'll be attracted to one person you'll want to share your life with. So just enjoy it and be curious.

What if no one is attracted to me?

There can be so much pressure on us to feel attractive, and sometimes you might feel the temptation to not be your true self in order to make someone be attracted to you, like using filters on social media, wearing lots of make-up or putting on an act and pretending to be someone you're not. But you can't keep up an act for ever so it makes much more sense to be yourself from the start. Let's face it, people are going to see you with no make-up or filter at some point. It's far better to have someone attracted to the real you, and remember, attraction isn't all about looks. A person could be attracted to your intelligence, your humour or how kind you are. There are so many different reasons someone might like you. And never forget, the most important relationship you will ever have is with yourself.

Dr Zoe's Prescription

Non-physical attraction

Identify three non-physical things that people could find attractive about you. For example, your kindness, humour, your baking skills! Then do this same exercise on someone you know. What could you find attractive about them apart from their looks?

Romantic relationships

Sometimes an attraction to someone else can be deeper than a crush and develop into your first romantic relationship. Often our first relationship can be with someone who was previously a friend and this can be a mixture of confusing and uncomfortable *and* exciting and thrilling.

Our first romantic relationships can be really tricky to navigate but there are some easy ways to tell if a relationship is healthy or not.

Signs of a healthy relationship

- They make you feel relaxed, calm and safe
- You can trust them
- You can be your true self and not have to pretend to be anything else
- They treat you the way you want to be treated
- You have good, open communication

Signs of an unhealthy relationship

- They make you feel anxious or nervous
- They make fun of you
- They take advantage of you, like asking for money
- They try to make you do things you don't want to do

If you are in an unhealthy relationship or know someone who is, it's really important to get support so that you can find the courage to end it.

I was once in a relationship with someone who I found out was cheating on me. I should have ended it the minute I found out, but your first love can be so intense, it can feel like you can't live without them. So I didn't break up with him immediately and with hindsight I can see that this caused me a lot more unnecessary pain.

The fact is we can't control how other people might treat us, and sometimes we're going to get hurt. But we can always control how we respond. And the best way to respond to an unhealthy relationship is to get out as soon as you can and to treat yourself with love and compassion.

- Tell a parent, carer or other trusted adult what is going on
- Contact Childline or a school counsellor for advice
- If you feel nervous about ending the relationship in person, it's fine to end it via message
- If you do end it in person, do it in a public place, and perhaps have a friend waiting nearby for moral support
- If they keep trying to get back with you or threaten you in any way, tell an adult or contact the police

CHAPTER 7

MENTAL HEALTH AWARENESS

Our mental health is just as important to maintain as our physical health, but sometimes people can feel embarrassed asking for help. Which is strange, because if you fell and sprained your wrist, you wouldn't feel ashamed about going to see a doctor, right? So why don't we apply the same thinking to our mental health? Just as some physical injuries won't heal on their own, we sometimes need help for problems with our mental health and there's absolutely no shame in reaching out and asking for help.

What is a mental health problem?

First of all, it's really important to get clear on what a mental health problem is. In life we will all experience a whole range of feelings and emotions. Sometimes we'll feel happy, sometimes sad, sometimes nervous, sometimes excited, and that's perfectly normal. Depression and anxiety are two of the most common mental health issues young people experience. So how do you determine when feelings of sadness are actually depression and feelings of nervousness are anxiety?

Sadness

Sadness is a totally normal emotion we all experience when something happens that hurts or upsets us. Feeling sad is nothing to worry about – in fact, it's a healthy way to process painful events. You might feel sad at something you watch online or on TV or because your favourite team didn't win at the weekend, but the next day you feel a lot better.

Depression

Depression is when you feel sad and low for a very long time. You tend to stop enjoying the things you used to find fun, and you might feel less like being around other people. It can also affect sleep, making you sleep a lot more or a lot less. The same is true with appetite, which depression can cause to go up or down.

Anxiety

Anxiety is your body's reaction to stressful or scary situations. We all feel anxious from time to time; we can't help it. Our bodies are wired up to respond in this way. But anxiety becomes a mental health issue when you feel nervous, worried and afraid to the point where it stops you being able to live your life normally or the way you want to. Sometimes people have physical symptoms of anxiety such as palpitations, shaking, panic attacks and sweating.

Panic attacks

A panic attack is when the body's natural response to stress or fear becomes exaggerated. They usually come on with no warning, making them even scarier. Symptoms of a panic attack include . . .

- Breathlessness
- Palpitations
- Sweating
- Chest pain
- Nausea
- Dizziness

There are lots of different types of anxiety – such as phobias, OCD, PTSD, body dysmorphic disorder and social anxiety disorder.

If you experience anxiety or panic attacks, there is a great breathing exercise later in this chapter that can really help.

Living with anxiety, depression or any other mental health issue can be difficult and can manifest itself in different ways. Here are some symptoms to look out for in yourself and others . . .

Emotional symptoms

- Feeling very sad and tearful all the time
- Feeling anxious
- Anger
- Mood swings, from high to low for no reason
- Worrying
- Exaggerated or unusual fears
- Difficulty paying attention
- Lethargy
- Sleeping problems

Physical symptoms

- Headaches
- Tummy aches
- Heart beating quickly
- Sweating
- Diarrhoea or feeling sick
- An increase or decrease in appetite
- Dry mouth

Behavioural symptoms

- Losing interest in hobbies and activities
- Not wanting to see your friends
- Spending more time on your own
- Your performance at school or in sports or other activities deteriorating
- Consuming or posting social media content that's dark, sad or self-critical
- Thinking about yourself negatively

Warning: what follows may be upsetting for some readers and is best read with an adult.

Mental health issues can sometimes also cause people to self-harm or have suicidal thoughts.

Self-harm can come in many different forms but the most common is cutting. It can be common in young people who might feel like it releases pent-up emotions their brains can't articulate. But at the very minimum it causes lifelong scarring and doesn't actually help the person get to the heart of the issue that is troubling them. If you are self-harming or know of anyone who is, talk to a trusted adult or seek help through the resources at the end of this book.

Suicide is when someone takes their own life. Many people worry that *talking* about suicide might make it more likely to happen, but this absolutely isn't true – it can actually save them. In most cases, suicidality – thoughts about suicide – doesn't lead to people taking their own lives but it can be very sad and indicate that someone needs help in addressing what is making them feel so low.

If you are having suicidal thoughts, know that you're not on your own and it's really important to speak to someone and let them know how you're feeling. Life might seem so bad at the moment that you feel like it's not worth living, but it always gets better. Please don't suffer in silence.

And if you're worried about someone else who's experiencing suicidal thoughts, you are absolutely allowed to let them know that you're worried about them. Tell a trusted adult or reach out for help on one of the hotlines at the end of this book.

When to seek help

It's important to realise that we will all sometimes experience these symptoms for a few hours or even a few days. But if you find yourself experiencing any of them for longer than a couple of weeks, speak to a parent, teacher or your GP. If you don't want a parent present, you can make an appointment to see your doctor on your own and it will be absolutely confidential. They'll only tell your parent if they feel you're in danger.

In my late teens I experienced some very difficult things. I didn't get the grades I needed to go to medical school, and I was going out with someone who wasn't very good for me. When we broke up, I found it very difficult.

I felt as if I'd lost my sense of direction and purpose. All of the things that made me feel safe and stable had been taken away. I felt very lost and afraid and unsafe. So I went through a period of quite bad depression.

I eventually sought help and was prescribed antidepressants, which helped a lot. After about six months things had really changed for the better, so I was able to come off the medication and I've never needed it again since. The antidepressants helped me get through the dark tunnel I was in and see the light at the end. But it's not the only way that depression can be treated. If you're experiencing depression, it's important you contact your local GP and discuss the options. They might recommend counselling, where you talk to a professional about what's on your mind, or they might initially suggest you find ways of alleviating stress and taking time for some self-care.

Another mental health issue I've experienced is anxiety. I've always been an anxious person; I was very clingy as a child, and super nervous whenever I was competing in races or dance competitions. It wasn't until I was a doctor that I realised I had clinical anxiety. I'd been getting various physical symptoms like palpitations and my oesophagus tightening, which was giving me pains in my chest. Sometimes it even felt as if my heart had stopped. It was very scary. As a doctor, I thought I had a stomach or heart problem. But a conversation with a friend helped me see that I was actually suffering from anxiety. She asked me when I got my symptoms and I realised that they only ever happened when I was stressed or when I was lying in bed at night worrying about things. I never got them during exercise or when I was feeling relaxed and happy.

I went to see my doctor, who prescribed me some anti-anxiety medication. But I also had some talking therapy and turned to exercise, which helped enormously. Every time I felt that tightening feeling, I'd go for a run or get active. It was like a form of medicine for me that I could prescribe whenever I needed it.

How to help your mental health

Talk to someone

If you think you're suffering from a mental health issue, the first step should always be talking to someone about how you're feeling, whether that's a grown-up or a mature and understanding sibling

143

or friend. Getting how you've been feeling off your chest can help a lot and hopefully the person you confide in will be able to offer you support and advice.

Exercise

Exercise can be anything that gets your heart beating a bit faster and gets you a little sweaty, so you don't have to be into sport to get the mental health benefits. Going for a walk, dancing around your bedroom, playing with younger siblings and gardening with your grandparents can all help.

Anything that gets you a little out of breath releases a cocktail of chemicals in your brain that make you feel better. These include endorphins, which are natural pain relievers, serotonin, which is the 'happy hormone', dopamine, which lights up the reward centre in your brain and makes you more confident, and noradrenalin, which makes you feel more energetic. Exercise can also be good for meeting new people and finding your tribe, and studies have shown that it can be just as effective as anti-depressants and talking therapy.

Mindfulness

Being mindful is all about living in the present moment. We spend so much time worrying about the past or future, but if you're able to come back to the present, things can seem a whole lot better.

Dr Zoe's Prescription

The five senses

One way to come back to the present is through your senses. Wherever you are right now, think about five things you can see. Then think about four things you can feel, such as the shoes on your feet, any slight breeze and the clothes on your body. Then think about three things you can hear, such as your breathing and the birds outside. Next, think about two things you can smell, like something close by you or your own skin. Finally think of one thing you can taste, which could be toothpaste or the last thing you ate. The great thing about this exercise is that you can do it anywhere – in a classroom, during an exam or on the bus!

Meditation

Meditation is another great way to calm your mind and body and come back to the present moment. Try this simple meditation the next time you're feeling anxious or stressed . . .

- Sit in a comfortable upright position
- Close your eyes and focus on your breathing
- Breathe in slowly through the nose and out through the mouth
- Picture a bright blue sky high above you
- Every time you have a thought, picture it as a cloud floating up out of your head and into the sky
- Feel yourself letting go of the thought as it drifts far away
- Repeat with any new thoughts you have and keep breathing deeply and slowly

Being in nature

Multiple studies have found that being in nature is hugely beneficial for our mental health, so go for regular walks in your local park and drink in the trees and plants and the sound of the birdsong.

Journaling

Journaling about how you're feeling is another great tool, especially if you're not sleeping well. Offload on to the page whenever you're feeling anxious, down or stressed and before you go to bed. It's amazing how therapeutic pouring your emotions out in this way can be.

Try using these journaling prompts to get started:
- I get really anxious/unhappy when . . .
- It makes me feel like . . .
- Three ways I could help myself feel better are . . .
- Three things that I am grateful for today

Diet

Did you know that your gut and your brain are very closely linked and send chemical signals to each other all the time? A few years ago a study showed that the types of food we eat can impact on our mental health. Basically, if the friendly bacteria that live in our gut are happy, they send signals to the brain which in turn make us feel happier. So what makes these gut bacteria happy? They love lots of fruit and veg and unprocessed foods, and probiotics, such as yoghurts, certain cheeses, kombucha, sauerkraut and kimchi, and prebiotics, such as beans, lentils and wholegrain bread and rice. The different gut bacteria also thrive on different food, so adding things like tins of mixed beans to curries, bolognese and soups; lots of different vegetables to stir fries; and mixed dried fruits to porridge, other cereal or salads really keeps them and us happy!

Sleep hygiene

Getting enough sleep is crucial to your mental health, so use the guidelines from chapter 4 to help you create a healthy sleep routine.

Breathing

If you're feeling stressed, panicked or out of control, one of the quickest ways to bring yourself back to a calm state is through your breathing. My favourite breathing technique is one that's used by Navy Seals in stressful situations – and they face some VERY stressful situations – and it's called box breathing.

- Look at something that's roughly box-shaped or imagine a box in front of you
- As you look up one side of the box, inhale for four seconds
- As you look across the top of the box, hold your breath for four
- As you look down the other side, exhale for four
- And as you look along the bottom hold for four

If you repeat this exercise for a minute, it can bring you out of stress and into calm, so it's great before an exam, or if you're running late, or if you've had an argument with your parents. You can do it in bed if you're feeling anxious and can't sleep. I sometimes use box breathing when I'm between patients and feeling stressed. It really helps me to reset and be my best self for my next patient.

Be a mental health first-aider

If you're reading this and currently experiencing poor mental health, know that you're not alone. Hopefully this chapter will have given you a better understanding of what you're going through and some tools to help you help yourself and others.

And it's so important that we help others. If you have a gut feeling that someone you know is struggling mentally, you're probably right, so don't be afraid to ask them how they are – how they *really* are – and give them the space to tell you.

A lovely side effect of helping others is that it makes us feel better about ourselves. So being a mental health first aider really is a . . .

 # WIN-WIN!

CHAPTER 8

WELCOME TO YOUR BEST LIFE!

We've covered a lot in this book and I know all the changes you're going through can feel daunting, but they're leading to something great.

Puberty is like the first chapter in a really exciting adventure called Growing Up, and in the last chapter of this book I want to show you how you can make the adventure of your life as happy and successful as possible.

Dr Zoe's recipe for living your best life

I believe there are three main ingredients when it comes to a happy and successful life:

- **Hard work** – regardless of background everyone has to work hard to achieve success

- **Aspirations** – whatever you think you'd like to achieve, aim just that little bit higher and you could end up exceeding your wildest dreams

- **Opportunities** – we might not be able to control what opportunities come our way but we all have control over being able to spot them – so if a door gets slammed in your face, go round the side and see if there's a window open, just like I did when I went to uni

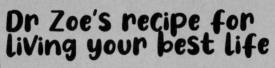

But what if you don't have as many opportunities as others because you come from a less privileged background?

Social privilege

In America, a university professor decided to do an experiment. He lined up his students on a start line for a race. But before he blew the whistle, he called out some statements. If the statements applied to the students, they were are allowed to take two steps forward. If the statements didn't apply, they had to stay where they were. These statements included:

- Both of your parents are still married
- You grew up with a father figure in the home
- You had access to a private education
- You had access to a private tutor growing up
- You've never had to worry about your phone being shut off
- You've never had to help your parents with the bills
- You've never wondered where your next meal was going to come from

By the time the professor had read all the statements, some of the students were already close to the finish line. Then he asked them all to turn around so they could see how many of their classmates were still way behind them at the start.

The race began and once it was over, it was obvious that the winners didn't feel good about it because it wasn't a fair race.

This is a powerful demonstration of how privilege works in our society. Countless studies have shown that if you grow up experiencing some of the issues highlighted by the teacher's statements, it's harder to achieve academic or career success. It also shows that the person who wins in an unfair race isn't any better than the person who came last.

If you have grown up with certain privileges, it's so important that you're grateful for them and you're understanding of those who haven't been so fortunate.

If I'd taken part in that race, I would have been one of the students still on the start line as I grew up in a single parent family on benefits. Life is definitely more challenging when you don't come from a privileged background. But like me, you can still get to the finish line.

The good news is, the harder you have to work to get somewhere, the easier it is when you get there. As I always say to the young people I work with: *'It's not where you start that matters, it's where you end up.'*

Find a role model

A role model is someone we look up to because we really respect how they behave or what they've achieved, and we'd like to be like them too.

Maybe you already have a role model or two. If you don't, is there anyone you can think of who has the kind of life you'd like to be living one day?

Although a lot of us have famous role models – mine include Oprah Winfrey and the Williams sisters – I believe that the best and most powerful role models are those we actually know in real life.

My mum was a great role model for me when I was younger. She taught me the most important lesson in life – how to love and make others feel loved. My grandma was another great role model to me as

she was a midwife and inspired me to go into healthcare. Being a role model isn't just about what someone has achieved, it's about how they make you feel. My PE teacher was another great role model because she inspired me, gave me confidence and helped me really believe in my **yes, I can** mantra. And this in turn inspired me to want to pass it on – doing things like giving motivational talks to girls and writing this book.

And talking of this book, thank you so much for reading *You Grow Girl!* I hope it's made you realise that you're definitely not alone when it comes to going through puberty. And that, if you are finding aspects of growing up difficult, it's so important to talk to someone about what you're going through. Whether you talk to a friend, family member, teacher or doctor, opening up is the first step to sorting a problem.

If there's one thing I want you to remember it's to be as kind to yourself as you are to your loved ones. And if that annoying little troll inside your head ever pipes up to tell you you're not good enough, or smart enough, or pretty enough, or whatever enough, remember to zip his mouth shut and tell him thanks, but no thanks! You deserve kindness just as much as others do because you're unique, special and perfect.

If this book has helped you, I'd love it if you passed it on to a friend, and ask them to pass it on too. Let's spread the **yes, I can** mantra far and wide!

Resources

Mental health

Young Minds (youngminds.org.uk) and Childline (childline.org.uk) offer excellent mental health resources.

The website Beat (beateatingdisorders.org.uk) offers lots of resources for people struggling with eating disorders.

If you ever deel desperate, or like you might hurt yourself, you deserve help as soon as you need it. To talk with someone confidentially about how you feel, you can ring HOPELINEUK on 0800 068 4141 or the Samaritans on 116 123

Food poverty

Jack Monroe's website (cookingonabootstrap.com) is full of recipes where she breaks down exactly how much they cost to make.

The Trussell Trust is another great resource. You can find out how to get vouchers for food banks at their website (trusselltrust.org).

Bullying resources

The Anti-Bullying Alliance (anti-bullyingalliance.org.uk) is a group of organisations and individuals working together to stop bullying and create safer environments for young people.

The National Bullying Helpline (nationalbullyinghelpline.co.uk) provides assistance to individuals struggling with bullying issues.

General resources

The NHS (nhs.uk) is a good resource to look up any health conditions that you want to know more about.

Health for Kids (healthforkids.co.uk) is a website designed for kids to learn about how to be healthy – they have a section for grown-ups too.

Apps

The Smiling Mind app is great for mindfulness and is designed for children.

Chill Panda helps you manage stress and feel better using breathing techniques, yoga, exercise and calming games.

Calm Harm is an app that helps young people manage the urge to self-harm.

Move Mood helps young people manage behaviours linked to low mood or depression.

Clear Fear helps young people manage symptoms of anxiety.

Tellmi is a free, fully moderated app for young people, which provides peer support and expert help, so you never need to feel alone.

Glossary

acne: A condition where people have lots of spots on the skin, which is common in teenagers.

dysmenorrhea: The medical word for period pain.

eating disorders: Serious mental illnesses where people use disordered eating behaviour as a way to cope with difficult situations or feelings.

follicle: A small sac of fluid in the ovary that contains a developing egg.

menorrhagia: The medical word for heavy periods.

menstrual cycle: The monthly cycle of changes in a female's hormones, which affect her ovaries and the lining of the uterus and result in either a pregnancy or a period.

oestrogen: One of the main female sex hormones. While both females and males produce oestrogen, it plays a bigger role in the female body.

premenstrual syndrome (PMS): The name for the symptoms women can experience in the weeks before their period.

progesterone: One of the main female sex hormones. It's involved in pregnancy and is produced mainly in the ovaries.

Acknowledgements

Firstly, I want to acknowledge the wonderful team at Hachette who believed in me and trusted me to write this important book. Laura Horsley, Victoria Walsh and Kaltoun Yusuf, thank you for making the whole process so seamless. And thank you to the brilliant designers, Pippi Grantham-Wright and Kat Slack. A special huge thanks to Siobhan Curham, who kept me company every step of the way. You listened to my life story and my deepest secrets, and not only understood, but truly felt the emotions with me. There are certain sections of this book that I could not have got down on to paper without your help, so thank you immensely.

Huge thanks to Luna Valentine for making my words come to effervescent life with your beautiful and genius animations, I truly hope that every girl can find a character in the book that somehow resonates with them. I'd like to thank my management team, Blondelle, Jess and especially Louisa who went above and beyond, consulting her own pre-teen daughter and school friends for some co-creation elements of the book. So, thanks also to Paloma and friends. And to my own friends (and daughters) who I consulted: Helena, Coco and Annabel, Sarah Le Brocq, Dr Amiee Vyas and Dr Ellie Tait, my bestie, fellow GP and mum of girls.

Thank you to family, who have always believed in me and never tried to hold me back from chasing what sometimes seemed like the wildest of dreams. I would not have had the honour of writing this book had I not believed in myself and become the person that I am today. And I have many incredible friends to thank for their part in that, who have guided me, supported me, believed in me, celebrated with me through the great times and held my hand through the dark times. You know who you are! You are the family that I have chosen; I couldn't have found myself without you, and I love you dearly. And a special mention of Yvonne, my high-flying, high-energy angel, who departed this world far too young, but whose voice I will always hear in my head, and it makes me smile. And a final mention to the most important people in my life – Stuart and Lisbon. Re-visiting my younger years has made me even more grateful and appreciative of the love we have. As a little girl my biggest dream was to have a perfect little family. And now here we are! I love you.

So, to any girl reading this book, however difficult certain stages of life may seem, don't worry, one day you WILL get there.

YES, YOU CAN!